# PLAYING GOD IN THE MEADOW

## OTHER BOOKS FROM BRIGHT LEAF

*House Stories: The Meanings of Home in a New England Town*
BETH LUEY

*Bricklayer Bill: The Untold Story of the Workingman's Boston Marathon*
PATRICK L. KENNEDY AND LAWRENCE W. KENNEDY

*Concrete Changes: Architecture, Politics, and the Design of Boston City Hall*
BRIAN M. SIRMAN

*Williamstown and Williams College: Explorations in Local History*
DUSTIN GRIFFIN

*Massachusetts Treasures: A Guide to Marvelous, Must-See Museums*
CHUCK D'IMPERIO

*Boston's Twentieth-Century Bicycling Renaissance: Cultural Change on Two Wheels*
LORENZ J. FINISON

*Went to the Devil: A Yankee Whaler in the Slave Trade*
ANTHONY J. CONNORS

*At Home: Historic Houses of Eastern Massachusetts*
BETH LUEY

*Black Lives, Native Lands, White Worlds: A History of Slavery in New England*
JARED ROSS HARDESTY

*At Home: Historic Houses of Central and Western Massachusetts*
BETH LUEY

*Flight Calls: Exploring Massachusetts through Birds*
JOHN R. NELSON

*Lost Wonderland: The Brief and Brilliant Life of Boston's Million Dollar Amusement Park*
STEPHEN R. WILK

*I Believe I'll Go Back Home: Roots and Revival in New England Folk Music*
THOMAS S. CURREN

*Legends of the Common Stream*
JOHN HANSON MITCHELL

*Mind and Hearts: The Story of James Otis Jr. and Mercy Otis Warren*
JEFFREY H. HACKER

*The Combat Zone: Murder, Race, and Boston's Struggle for Justice*
JAN BROGAN

*Letters from Red Farm: The Untold Story of the Friendship between Helen Keller and Journalist Joseph Edgar Chamberlin*
ELIZABETH EMERSON

*Trail Running Eastern Massachusetts*
BEN KIMBALL

*A Union Like Ours: The Love Story of F. O. Matthiessen and Russell Cheney*
SCOTT BANE

# PLAYING GOD IN THE MEADOW

## HOW I LEARNED TO ADMIRE MY WEEDS

MARTHA LEB MOLNAR

BRIGHT LEAF
BOOKS THAT ILLUMINATE
Amherst and Boston
*An imprint of University of Massachusetts Press*

*Playing God in the Meadow* has been supported by the Regional Books Fund, established by donors in 2019 to support the University of Massachusetts Press's Bright Leaf imprint.

Bright Leaf, an imprint of the University of Massachusetts Press, publishes accessible and entertaining books about New England. Highlighting the history, culture, diversity, and environment of the region, Bright Leaf offers readers the tools and inspiration to explore its landmarks and traditions, famous personalities, and distinctive flora and fauna.


Printed in the United States of America

ISBN 978-1-62534-687-2 (paper); 688-9 (hardcover)

Designed by Deste Roosa
Set in Minion Pro and Chantal
Printed and bound by Books International, Inc.

Cover design by Deste Roosa
Cover photo by Johnny Caspari on Unsplash

Library of Congress Cataloging-in-Publication Data
A catalog record for this book is available from the Library of Congress.

British Library Cataloguing-in-Publication Data
A catalog record for this book is available from the British Library.

Chapters 7 and 8 were adapted from "Weed Wars: A Battle against Poison Parsnip," *Northern Woodlands* magazine, summer 2016, https://www.northernwoodlands.org.

*With gratitude to the earth,*
*from whom I have learned.*

# CONTENTS

# PREFACE

After decades of fantasizing, of working two jobs and practicing extreme fiscal responsibility, followed by a year of disappointing searching, we found our land.

It was not a promising first meeting. Atop a rusted cattle gate, a prominent sign threatened that "Trespassers Will Be Shot." The rutted remnants of tractor and truck tracks led past hundreds of apple trees in various stages of death and dying. Those still standing had been twisted into tortured shapes by all the pests and diseases known to apple trees in New England. The cows and bulls roaming the land had chewed the leaves off the lower limbs while voles and mice had stripped the bark.

Still, the grass was lush, reaching my chest. The wildflowers were as many and as high. We bushwhacked to the top of the hill, climbing over fallen limbs and trunks, shaking off grass and flower seeds, and sending up clouds of bobolinks and red-winged blackbirds that complained bitterly about the invasive humans.

It was a brilliantly clear September day, making all of creation visible. The Taconic Mountains, all soft shoulders, climbed in rows in along one side. Among them, Birdseye, a massive hump of steep rock face, brooded directly over us, flat against the sky, a dark cutout against the blue. The eroded southern hills were dotted with small tilted farms. A little white town sat in the valley on the other side, where gentle hills gave way to a long, narrow lake. Beyond that, the Adirondacks lined up in glistening peaks.

Above all hung the entire bowl of the sky, with high clouds streaming toward us. It was a big western sky, an engulfing and throbbing presence, a force that we later learned alternately bore down with massing weather, then retreated to a high and benevolent immensity.

We looked, turning in slow circles. We sat on a smooth ledge where no trees or grass grew and looked some more. The breeze brought the odor of animals and tough grass and tough wildflowers. The silence held all the sounds of earth and heaven. Together the smells and the silence carried all the acid and grit of Manhattan out of my soul.

There on the earth's hard bulk, I felt slight, a speck on the planet. And it was a good feeling, not of being lost but of being found. Here was unlimited sun and space, enough land for growing gardens of food and flowers, for solitude and long walks. A patch of land where I could control the chaos of the world and insulate my family from the earth's uncertain future. A home where I could care for the earth and be fed in return. Here was unspoiled nature that we would preserve in its magnificent state. No, improve it with even more wildflowers and native grasses, return it to its original, wild state. Here was deliverance from noise and nonsense, from the overbearing presence of the world. The insulation was thin, but real enough to offer respite from my history, to make putting down roots safe.

Within two months we were the exhilarated, joyful, terrified owners of forty acres of a dying hilltop orchard in south-central Vermont.

We put up a cabin and learned to live a simple life. Then we built a house, stamping the land with our presence. We didn't know what we had set in motion. We didn't know that our very presence would invite an army of interlopers to join the grasses and wildflowers on the hill. We didn't know that forces beyond us would upend our naive plans, forcing us to learn to accept and compromise. And we didn't know how we, too, would be transformed along with the land.

# PLAYING GOD IN THE MEADOW

# 1 FROM ORCHARD TO MEADOW

*I robbed the Woods—*
*The trusting woods . . .*
*My fantasy to please.*
—EMILY DICKINSON, "I robbed the Woods"

The orchard on our land was like the swimming pool that comes with a newly acquired house. And we were like the people who buy that house, not realizing the pool is not a bonus but a serious liability, a harbinger of endless labor, a dangerous presence, and a disincentive to future buyers. We bought our forty acres of a dying apple orchard having no understanding of what thousands of trees meant.

Oh, but those shiny Red Delicious apples were juicy, and their white flesh had an intensity of flavor such as I remembered from childhood apples, utterly absent from the anemic ones featured in food markets today. That is, after you managed to spit out or otherwise remove the apple maggots' brown tunnels and the scabs that reached to the core. Still, for the first few years, I made several pies out of the bushel we picked. Wandering among the rows, the late autumn sun falling through a lattice of leaves, warming my neck or thigh or an arm in turn, I would move slowly through the rows, imprisoned by trees on every side and losing my way. Walking up the hill would always be the way out, but I preferred to sit and, leaning on a peeling trunk, doze off.

It was an orchard, even if it was dying, and I still loved the thought of living in the middle of all the trees, hidden by the vastness of all those acres. Our land seemed enormous then and still does all these years later. But my husband, Ted, rightly insisted we had to seriously consider the options. Doing nothing while watching the orchard die was not a good one. Too depressing. Cutting it all down and starting fresh, with what was not clear, was radical but practical. Restoring it to a healthy orchard was daunting, barely imaginable.

"Cut the trees," advised our first friends in Vermont, who like us had bought an apple orchard, one they succeeded in restoring to a productive wonder. Why couldn't we turn our orchard around to look like theirs?

"Because," she said. "Just look at us." Then he catalogued their endless labor, detailing how the orchard took over their lives so they couldn't travel, how they had to house and care for seasonal workers, and worse, how they sank their life savings into a very risky investment.

"Is this what you want?" she asked.

Well, yes, we wanted our orchard to look like theirs, but without sacrificing the entirety of our planned new lifestyle, which included travel and more free time. The goal of semiretirement was to do less, not more.

"Cut the trees!" both repeated.

"Before you can't," he added. Once you start down the path of "saving" them, there's no stopping. There's no going back. You can't just let them be, let them die slowly. And you can't shrink your project. It's all or nothing. Forever. It's the damn orchard or your very life! Instead, they suggested planting a row of crab apples along the driveway that would flower even more impressively than our dying trees, which were, we agreed, also blocking the full 360-degree views that were sure to reveal themselves once the they were gone.

We knew they were right. You *can* grow terrific apples in New England, but it takes deep knowledge, serious commitment, and unremitting attention.

The history of apple trees explains a lot. The first seeds were brought from the fruit's origins in Central Asia to Europe. When the first European settlers arrived in the New World, they found only wild crab apples, but being planful, they had brought apple seeds with them. The earliest record of cultivated apples in New England appeared in 1623, just three years after the landing of the *Mayflower.*

The cultivated seeds mingled with the native crab apples, sprouting fruit with a dizzying combination of new flavors and characteristics. Today, some thirty to forty varieties are grown commercially in New England's six states, leading with McIntosh, followed by Cortland, Macoun, Empire, Gala, and Honeycrisp.

The diseases we found on our apples can be managed with chemicals, organically or with a combination of the two, a process called integrated pest management. All involve rigorous and complicated regimens, especially with trees as neglected and as far gone as ours. But the problems are multiplying even in healthy orchards. In recent years, a more devastating disease has been ravaging apple and pear orchards in our area. Called fire blight and caused by a bacterium, it can devastate a healthy orchard in a single season. The disease, which used to be easily managed by trimming diseased branches and spraying with antibiotics, is becoming more virulent as the climate changes and as growers plant trees more intensively to produce higher yields. The newer varieties may also be more vulnerable, some researchers say. The blight is becoming resistant to antibiotics—just as our human diseases respond less to antibiotics than in the past—and it has become more aggressive, wiping out thousands of trees in some places.

Ted and I had neither unremitting attention nor endless commitment, and no expertise, none, so after many discussions and several consultations with our orchardist friends, we arrived at the wrenching decision we knew we would eventually come to. We would cut the trees. Most of them anyway.

But now there was the question of how. I knew just enough to understand that it wouldn't be a burly lumberjack arriving from the backwoods, not even half a dozen of them with chainsaws to fell thousands of trees and haul them away. We could only hope that there was an efficient method and that we would discover it in time. But no matter what, cutting and removing the trees would involve lots of labor and large equipment, all of which would add up to lots of money we didn't have. I would do some digging on the Internet through the winter, talk to people, call the local extension service. The answers had to be out there. Meanwhile, we were enjoying picking more apples than we had use for, finally spreading them out for the deer. Then it was time to figure out how to get a cabin put up that would serve until the house would be built several years later.

In the midst of this confusion, and while being lost one day in the nearby city of Rutland, the answer came. It came all at once, just handed to us like an enormous gift-wrapped box presented for no reason at all. Rutland is not a large city by any standard, but I am good at being lost in a box, as my family and friends like to remind me while relishing once again the "unbelievable" stories about how I was lost in . . . It's true that I have graduated from being directionally challenged to being directionally disabled, but in this case, my disability turned out to have a silver, no, a solid gold lining.

I passed a sign for the US Department of Agriculture. I walked in, not expecting much, knowing nothing about the USDA except that it had to do with agriculture, and reasoning that apple trees are an agricultural crop. I was directed to a woman who congratulated me warmly on our move and asked what our plans were once we cut the trees.

Plans? We had no plans. Yes, we'll plant a vegetable garden and a perennial flower garden, but those would be near the house, leaving all the rest as a huge dying orchard. So what we needed to do was get the trees cut, which would leave us with . . . grass?

It would be a meadow, the woman assured me, nodding encouragingly.

A meadow! A meadow sounded romantic, dreamy. And not quite real.

But the woman, a part-time farmer and all business, continued to lay out the options, and I was forced to focus. If we agreed to have most of the trees cut, the land would quickly become a habitat for ground-nesting birds. It so happened that the USDA was looking to preserve such habitats, which were becoming rare, for the birds, which were also becoming rarer. The USDA would cover three-quarters of the cost of cutting the trees and brushhogging the resulting meadow once a year to keep trees from growing.

Really? That would be . . . a miracle, the answer I didn't even know we were seeking. But I was skeptical. What would we have to do to earn such gifts? Nothing at all. We would only have to sign a contract agreeing to maintain the resulting meadow as habitat for ground-nesting birds for five years. We would plant no trees, put up no buildings, nor cut the tall grass until after the baby birds had fledged and parents and babies had left on their odyssey to Argentina. Would we agree?

Would we? Would we? Yes, we would. Of course we would. How could we not? We signed the paperwork that very day, and Ted rushed back to deliver it before the office closed. We were overcome by the sheer luck we had stumbled upon. What if I hadn't been lost? Even disabilities can turn into unexpected gifts. Certainly this gift was unearned, pure serendipity.

A couple of months later, once the ground froze hard, a monstrous orange brontosaurus showed up, ridden by a silent young man who, after a meager greeting, turned off our driveway and into the orchard. Then, after he raised the brontosaurus's trunk to the first tree, I watched as it chewed up the top branches, lowered its trunk, and chewed up the tree down to below the thin snow. In less than five minutes, the tree was gone, its place marked by a small pile of fresh wood chips. In less than five minutes, man and machine moved to the next tree, and the one after that, hour after hour in the cold gunmetal air. They ground their way up the hill row by row, then down the hill. In a week, all the trees except four rows along the perimeter were gone. We would, in time, attempt to revive some of those. Meanwhile, they would serve as a vestige of what once was while the rest would become a meadow. That's what the USDA woman said, and I chose to believe her.

It was hard to imagine a thriving meadow.

The land was a wasteland of wood chips and a few remaining larger smashed tree parts that escaped the brontosaurus's jaws. There, exposed, lay the land's injured ribs, welts, clefts, and sockets, all its gashes laid open under the leaden winter sky. The ravage was complete. Decades of patient growth, of tenacious survival, were spit out on the denuded earth. Not just the trees; last fall's milkweed pods and dried goldenrod flowers, the tall grasses, even the nettles lay mashed into the ground. All was colorless, a sterile moonscape. I was devastated with regret and worry.

What, I wondered, will happen to the seeds of the grasses and flowers, to the wild strawberries and blackberries that lay dormant, now smashed under the brontosaurus? To the burrows of small animals, the mice, shrews, and snakes that had lived under the trees for decades? To the brown rabbit that would sit in front of our cabin, unafraid of these never-before-seen large, giggling creatures? To the billions of unseen organisms that inhabit every cubic inch of earth? There was a whole universe of interdependence between the trees, the microorganisms on their roots, and the insects. What if we had thoughtlessly, arrogantly launched a chain of death that would spiral into the extinction of this whole hill?

I suspected I was vastly exaggerating our impact. Left alone, the animals would wander back. The seeds would survive, the grass and flowers would return, the land would regenerate. Nature always yearns to return to its natural state. The orchard was not, after all, a natural landscape, having been planted and maintained by humans with machinery and chemicals. A rainy spring followed by a warm summer would work their magic. Crickets and fireflies would move in, and bees and butterflies would hover over the returning wildflowers. Yes, but . . . looking at the ravage during January's thaw as the thin snow that covered the destruction melted before noon, it was hard to believe in anything good coming out of the flattened wasteland.

Ignoring the evidence that stared back at me, I comforted myself through the long winter with visions of tall waving grass studded with brilliant flowers, and with flocks of birds moving into the new meadow to a welcoming home.

I was not a birder; in fact, I was barely aware of them. They were just there, part of the landscape. Only when the crows woke me on summer mornings or a seagull flew off with my sandwich did I take notice of them as sentient beings with needs and intelligence.

But when the first birds showed up, soon after the last snow melted and the grass was already pushing up powerful stems, I was a changed person. These birds were not just heard, up high in the trees, falling silent as I came close; they were there, right there, all around me. The air throbbed with their shrieking, piping calls. The red-winged blackbirds and robins hung out at the birdbath in the center of the lawn where I could see them from everywhere inside the house and every time I stepped out. They hung out not by ones or twos but by dozens, coming and going, calling and arguing, turning the place into a hub of frantic activity. When I threw the sunflower seeds I put in salad onto the lawn, these birds were joined by the blue jays and chickadees that had stayed around all winter but I had hardly noticed. They mobbed the patch, pecking, chasing, returning. The tree swallows swooped and dived and soared all around me on their acrobatic hunts for insects in the air. I rushed out to buy a bird feeder and bird food, which brought ever more birds. And before I had time to learn more than the names of these few birds, there was frantic activity in what was rapidly turning into a meadow. The bobolinks had arrived!

Walking out on a May morning to get water from the rain barrel, there were new sounds in the grass. Not just the ordinary bird cheep of robins and the harsh call of red-winged blackbirds. This was a bubbly sound, rising and falling, a deliriously cheerful melody, one I still hear as a drunken song. Then I saw one and another, bobbing on the tallest grass stems. Elegant birds, decked out in glossy black and white feathers like a backward tuxedo, with puffy yellow heads, forming a morning cocktail party. Bobolinks, of course. They were scolding me, the large invader in what they came to regard as their territory over a single night.

They were expected; they were, after all, directly responsible for the meadow. But I had never seen or heard one before; I didn't know they would be so beautiful, nor that their song would be so intoxicating. In the coming days, I would note that the birds I saw were only the emissaries, the alpha males that came ahead to scout homesites. New waves would arrive, until the infant meadow was a rushing, brimming, calling, metropolis with the bravest bobolinks painting arabesques in the air above the grass.

But the show was, and is even more so today, a mirage of plenty. Because, as I was learning, ground-nesting birds are in dire need of habitat. Like their woodland songbird cousins, they are caught in a perfect human-made storm in both their winter homes in the tropics and in their summer homes in our New England fields.

Bobolinks were once the monarchs of meadows. Today their numbers are plummeting; their population is shrinking by over 2 percent a year since 1966, a massive decline.

Bobolinks spend the winter in South America, mostly Argentina, an astounding 6,200-mile trip for the one-ounce birds.

The average bobolink travels the equivalent of four to five times around the world in a lifetime. But things are tough for them once they arrive in Argentina. Pesticides are used on rice and other grains that the bobolinks (sometimes called "rice bird" for their tendency to feed on cultivated grains) eat. A single seed coated in neonicotinoids, now the most commonly used pesticide on earth, can kill a bird. Birds that frequent agricultural fields are particularly vulnerable. Development in Brazil, as in the rest of the world, is also shrinking the available habitat.

Things are not better when they return to our fields. Bobolinks build their nests, lay their eggs, and raise their young in the long grass, but long-grass meadows are in very short supply. Where once, in the mid-1800s, Vermont was 80 percent fields and 20 percent forest, it's now the reverse. Furthermore, most of the remaining fields are used for haying, and to get the best quality hay, the fields are now cut two or three times a season. Which means that an entire season of breeding is shredded in the blades.

It's not just a question of habitat; climate change is also complicating things for bobolinks and all other migrating birds. Spring comes earlier, so by the time the birds arrive, the food sources they depend on during their long trip and at their destination are already gone. The plants have already bloomed and the berries have shriveled.

I have been witnessing the decline firsthand. For the first few years of our meadow's life, a walk in early summer would send up clouds of these birds, filling the air with soaring beauty and jubilant song. The same walk now sends up fewer birds, and their music, still jubilant and soaring, sometimes sounds like a mournful dirge to my oversensitized ears.

We often invite people to visit us during the height of the bobolinks' breeding season. They come in late May when the bobos are at their most protective of the just-laid eggs, performing the liveliest aerial displays and loudest singing. We walk the cut paths through the tall shining grass, where the buttercups and bluets wink, and birds rise into the warm air from invisible nests in the grass. Everyone is steeped in pure joy.

Should I then mention that there used to be more, many more bobolinks? Should I tell them, as they turn their smiling faces to the fields and back to me, so grateful, that just six or seven years ago, bluebirds always flew out of their nests in the old apple trees, never failing to shock us with their lavender wings and apricot chests? So exotic they should be in some tropical rainforest, I would always think, not up here. Should I break the spell of what passes for plenty, for life overflowing, and cite percentages and fractions of loss and despair? I don't. Not then. We're alive and here with the bobolinks, the lucky ones who are also alive, walking among them on this perfect morning.

Some efforts to rescue the bobolinks look promising.

The Bobolink Project, based at the University of Vermont and the University of Connecticut, is one creative approach. It seeks pledges from donors to pay farmers to leave fields uncut until the birds leave. Similar programs exist or are being considered in other states, including New Jersey, Rhode Island, and Massachusetts, and in Ontario in Canada. Clearly, I'm not the only one to fall in love with bobolinks. Still, these efforts are far too little.

The red-winged blackbirds that mob our bird feeder from March onward lack the bobolinks' musical talents. Theirs is a nasal "conk-a-ree!" Nonetheless, it's a most welcome sound since they are the first to return, signaling the beginning of spring. Males are glossy black with scarlet shoulder patches bordered in yellow, like fancy military epaulettes. The males spend much of the breeding season sitting on a high grass perch guarding their territories and singing their hearts out. The far less dramatic streaky brown females tend to slink through the grasses collecting food and nest material, seemingly unaware of the sentries above them. Red-winged blackbirds are common, with an estimated population of one hundred fifty million. But their numbers are also in decline due to the same factors that are causing the bobolinks' shrinking numbers. Unless we pay attention, we'll soon have to launch programs to save these iconic grassland birds too.

American goldfinches return after the redwings but before the bobolinks. They flit between the birdbath and the feeder, flashing lemon-yellow sunshine. Small birds, they live in open areas with shrubs and trees, but appear happy enough to live in our meadow and eat whatever I and the meadow offer.

Can wild birds be pets? With hummingbirds, the answer is "almost." Which is why I anticipate their arrival more than that of any others.

Although they build their nests in trees and not in the grass, I lump them with "my" birds for no reason other than I love them as much or maybe a little more. And if I stretch the logic a bit, while they don't build their nests in the grass, they do so in the tall shrubs in the grass and visit the wildflowers in the meadow for nectar as much as the sugar water I put out for them. This makes hummingbirds a kind of meadow denizen.

They arrive on a day in May. I'm busy with the garden and not thinking hummingbirds at all. I go into the kitchen to grab lunch, and find three or four of them following my movements through the windows. I drop whatever I'm holding, and signaling to Ted to come look, I rush to retrieve the dusty glass feeders. While they wait patiently by the windows for me to come out with their sugar water, we have a conversation.

"Welcome, welcome, you gorgeous creatures!" I call through the windows as they track my every move. One hangs in front of the window over the sink as I fill the pot to boil their water, his wings rotating at a blinding tempo, waiting silently, staying put. When I step out to hang the feeders, they hover at a polite distance, but when I step away, the standard battle begins. Each bird insists on getting a feeder all to himself and refusing to share. This battle is followed by many others, each and every day, because hummers are not sharing creatures. Despite their glowing prismatic plumage, their diminutive size, and all-around gorgeousness, they are not nice birds, being shockingly aggressive. We watch their battles and war dances, and sometimes cringe to hear the body slams these tiny birds, weighing a quarter of the weight of a nickel, inflict on each other. I have seen them attack blue jays and even go after a crow.

There are many hummingbirds and they run out of food daily, so I'm kept happily busy. But they do say thank you, repeatedly. If I happen to be sitting still, one or another comes up to hover in front of my face. They do this interspecies examination all summer long, but just before they leave for the season, the hovering and staring are especially drawn out. Two or three of them, one at a time, hover a foot from my nose as I smile silently, quivering with pleasure and disbelief. It may back away a few feet, flying backward as hummingbirds can, only to return and hover some more. They are saying thank you and goodbye. I know this because they are saying it to me only, not to Ted, because I'm the one who feeds them. The next day they are gone. But not gone from my thoughts. I am bereft and anxious. Will they survive the journey to Argentina?

What kinds of threatening changes will they encounter on their route? What about the killing threats of their winter grounds, and finally the thousands of perilous miles returning here?

"A person with an ecological education lives alone in a world of wounds," observed environmentalist Aldo Leopold. I read this many years ago. Before we had meadows with birds in them. Before we had thriving meadows that I knew were threatened. Before we had magnificent meadows whose evolving life encompassed the whole world writ small.

# 2 BUGS

It wasn't only birds I learned to appreciate once we moved to the hill. I also learned to like insects. Some of them at least. Sort of.

Once, I could ignore insects. But then Ted and I moved into our first apartment, which happened to share a wall with the garbage chute through which all the tenants in the midsize building dropped their trash. Then they could forget about it. We could not. Ever forget. The wall, being old, was breached by innumerable cockroaches that moved into our tiny studio apartment. And stayed. They came in shades of brown and black and ranged from the size of a large ant to a small mouse.

It was a traumatic year. For decades after we moved out of that apartment, I never put on a pair of shoes without first checking carefully for reclusive roaches.

I knew little about insects that were not roaches, that lived outdoors and didn't climb into your shoes. The familiar ones—ants, flies, mosquitoes—did nothing to endear the insect world to me.

There is something repulsive about insects. Their extreme difference from us, their absolute weirdness. Too many legs, too many eyes. They wear their skeletons outside their bodies. They skitter, they fly, they land on you, they bite. There are too many of them and they invade what I see as my turf.

I'm not alone. There's a reason insects are featured prominently in horror movies. And a reason they never grace cereal boxes and are never, ever turned into soft and furry stuffed spittlebugs or house flies. In a recent survey of fears conducted at Chapman University in Orange, California, a quarter of respondents said they were afraid of insects. Their fear landed just below fear of natural disasters, theft, and public speaking, and higher than becoming unemployed or getting mugged. There is actually a word for extreme fear and disgust of insects: entomophobia.

Living in the meadow, I have had to make peace not only with the bees and butterflies, which everyone adores, but also with hoverflies, assassin bugs, and striped, iridescent, or spotted beetles, and a host of millipedes and worms, slugs and caterpillars. Working in the earth, I am reminded that a single square yard of soil contains five hundred to two hundred thousand individual arthropods, which covers all of the above and then some. There are in fact more than forty tons of insects for every human being on the planet. If all the insects got together, they could crush us . . . like a bug.

I have been moving from fear and loathing to brave acts.

One fall I removed a huge and magnificent wasp nest so my grandson could take it to school for show-and-tell. (In the interest of full disclosure, the wasps were absent, it being late fall.) And rather than running from bees, I now lean into the flower cup to watch a huge bumblebee cover itself with yellow pollen. At the lake, I sit still, waiting for dragonflies to land on me. Once, with my in-house human insect remover unavailable, I lifted an outsize grasshopper off the kitchen floor with my bare hands and calmly took it outside. Grasshoppers happen to be harmless and an intense green. But they are all toes and knees and bulging eyes. Still too weird.

This radical change was not a quick transformation. It was helped along with learning about the crucial services insects provide. They pollinate some three-quarters of the crops we rely on as food, a service worth as much as $577 billion every year. They act as sanitation experts, breaking down waste so the world doesn't become overrun with dung. The good guys among them help keep the bad guys in check in our gardens and farms. They aerate the soil and recycle nutrients. Simply, the earth would starve and rot without insects. Which is a frightening thought given that insects populations are in free fall. Which still doesn't make me like them exactly. More like grudging acceptance mingled with appreciation.

# 3 FRAGMENT OF PARADISE

*No creature is fully itself till it is, like the dandelion, opened in the bloom of pure relationship to the sun, the entire living cosmos.*

—D. H. LAWRENCE, "Reflections on the Death of a Porcupine"

Carrying two wildflower guidebooks, I am wandering up and down the hill, now almost empty of apple trees. The land is rapidly, miraculously turning into a nascent meadow, the grass rushing to fill the empty spots where trees had stood. It's May, and the empty spots have disappeared, along with the small and large wood chips that had been trees just months before. With no input from us, with no help or coaxing, the orchard is rapidly becoming what I imagine prairies look like in spring. Prairie in the Midwest is a meadow in New England. So we have a meadow.

The guidebooks include dandelions in all its varieties, of which there are more than I imagined. Does that mean dandelions are wildflowers? Surely not. Dandelions are the bane of anyone bent on creating a living green carpet known as a lawn. One of the guidebooks does note that dandelions are alien, while the other refers to it as a common European weed. Likewise clover, noted as alien but spread over several pages in one of the books. But why include dandelion and clover in wildflower books? Aren't wildflowers supposed to be pretty and pretty rare?

Dandelion and clover are ubiquitous in our meadow. Clover is especially prevalent in the oval piece of earth that surrounds the house and which Ted mows more regularly than strictly necessary, because despite his vehement denial, he actually likes mowing. He loves sitting on his little tractor, a huge step up from the enormous push mower he used at our previous house. I watch him astride the tractor, his ears sporting huge red earphones, his face a wide smile, as he scoots around in concentric circles, then fills in the middle with straight lines. Our lawn is robust but far from perfect, consisting of whatever happened to grow under the apple trees, including a large percentage of clover, now shorn short.

He is mowing right now, and I walk away from the noise toward a far corner of the property toward the small forest that occupies the top half of the triangular piece of land.

The meadow glistens in the sharp light of the storm-scoured morning. The starkness of the torn-up landscape has given way to a riot of throbbing life, nature reclaiming the devastation perpetrated by the brontosaurus. Bees swarm the dandelions, the clover, the wild strawberries, the violets. The grass is a wilderness of shoots, stems, leaves, drinking sunlight, rain, air. As thick and glossy as an animal's pelt, it gives the lie to the dullness of watching grass grow. It has a will of its own. Untilled, unweeded, unmanaged, crawling with iridescent beetles, with snakes and voles. It's powerful, unmanageable, disorderly, the antithesis of a pesticided, herbicided lawn.

The mountains radiate the deep burgundy of maple flowers. The nearby low hills sport new leaves in every shade of green ever known and many yet unnamed, because we don't have nearly enough words in English for spring's profusion of greens.

Most dazzling and most shameless are the flowers. Even these meek spring blooms are blatantly sexual. Flowers live for sex. A flower is a sex organ with an ovary and a male stamen with pollen, which must make its way into the ovary to fertilize it. For this, help is needed. So flowers enlist pollinators that fly, crawl, and walk, seducing them primarily with colors, brilliant to us and even more so to insects, who see colors through the ultraviolet range that is invisible to us. Demure white and cream flowers stand out as much as the loud ones, but they do so in the dark, attracting bats and moths. Some, like our wild roses and iris, even offer landing strips on their petals, inviting tired insects to take a break, and when they leave, to carry the pollen with them to another flower.

Warmth is another tool flowers use. The unloved skunk cabbage that we see in any damp area in early spring stays between fifty-nine and seventy-two degrees for two weeks in February and March, even while sitting on a ring of melting snow. Philodendron plants in Brazil maintain 115 degrees in fifty-degree temperature. To insects craving warmth, these plants are irresistible.

Some flowers' intoxicating or sickening (to us) aromas also beguile insects. Some smell like food to their pollinators. That's how the Venus flytrap lures insects into its ingenious trap. Others smell like the sex pheromones of insects or like excrement or like a rotting corpse. Insects revel in the carrion odor of black cohosh, which in late summer light up our forests with their white spikes.

Nectar, the sugary liquid glistening at the bottom of an open flower, is as irresistible to animals as fine chocolate is to us. If that's not incentive enough, flowers spike it up—nectar has recently been found to contain a jolt of caffeine and a touch of nicotine. We don't know if bees get a buzz, but experiments show they prefer the caffeinated version.

Some liaisons can be deadly. One orchid attaches its pollinium—lumps of coagulated pollen—to the eye of the moth that pollinates it. Others attach the pollinium to the tongues of birds, which is clearly deadly, as it prevents the birds from eating. Our local flowers use more mundane murder weapons. Gnats that enter jack-in-the-pulpit can escape if they enter a male flower, but are trapped and die in female flowers. Once they've delivered the sought-after pollen from the male flower, which fertilizes the female flower, their job is done and they're rewarded with a slow death.

Walking through the fields later in the season, I become covered with clinging burrs and sticky seeds; I too have been recruited to carry seeds of bedstraw and clover. I pick them off, but what of the furry voles and rabbits? And imagine the porcupines!

Not all flowers are femmes fatales. Grasses and most trees bear barely visible blossoms that depend on the wind for dispersion. This saves the plants the enormous energy required to put on a showy display and generate complicated aromas. Instead, they produce astounding numbers of seeds to ensure that a few are blown to an optimal spot.

But I prefer the blousey lovelies around me as I plod toward the still-pale blackberries, hoping for a few that have surged ahead of schedule.

I think of my mother more often on this hill than I did during the early years after her death when we were still living in a New York City suburb. I think about how she would have loved this place, loved it with more passion than even I can muster because she was a more passionate person. One of her chief passions was Nature with a capital "N" because it encompassed everything, from flowers, trees, and skies to dogs, birds, and plums.

She was a poet, unschooled, unsophisticated, but driven to write verse. During the nine months she spent in Auschwitz, she composed poems in her head and memorized them. Years later, she was able to recall these poems and write them down. Many, more than would seem natural under the circumstances, were about the trees she saw leafing out in May through the slats of the cattle car. About her memories of birds in the trees surrounding the large church she used to pass on the way to school. About the lilacs by the outhouse, and the explosive growth of the cabbages in the only vegetable garden she had ever seen in the city where she grew up.

I have often wondered about why some people respond so powerfully to the natural world while others are oblivious. Is the response innate or learned?

My mother lived most of her life in cities but longed for the open country. My father grew up in a village and moved to the city as a teenager, and lived in cities the rest of his life. He had no affinity for the country. When Ted and I moved to our suburban house, an ugly house we bought because it was surrounded by acres of forest, he was horrified. "Why so many trees? And no street lights? What are you going to do with so many trees and no people?" He was intensely interested in people. Trees and all they implied were distractions from what made the world fascinating and safe.

Until I was nine, my family lived in Cluj, a midsize city in Romania, on a street lined with huge chestnut trees. Not far was the city's main park, an eastern European version of formal French landscape design, with wide boulevards for strolling, dandelions for stringing into necklaces and tiaras, and a lake for boating and ice skating. I loved all these places, tame and safe, with clearly defined borders, which were nevertheless so much more thrilling than life inside our house or relatives' houses, where the adults talked and talked about incomprehensible but terrible things, about Auschwitz, a faraway place I had never been to, about the *lager*, and selections, and a little girl cousin, and another boy cousin who were "taken."

It was our garden, shady and damp, hidden from the street by a stone fence and overgrown shrubs, that offered a daily haven.

Romania in the 1950s was an impoverished country, squeezed under the Soviet thumb. My father had managed, through bold bribery, to retain his tailoring shop and employ two or three apprentices. We were therefore better off than most. Our house was relatively large and had hot running water. Our pantry was filled with shelves heavy with glossy preserved fruit, and we had meat several times a week. On special occasions, I was given chocolates and oranges, imported from exotic places and secured through not entirely legal means. As the first girl born into the remnant of our extended family, I was a symbol of survival and regeneration, and more than that. A miracle, utterly spoiled and endlessly loved.

Still, there was no television, virtually no toys, and just a couple of picture books. I was an only child until I was six, and there were very few children among the Holocaust survivors who made up our extended family and my parents' social circle. School didn't start until the age of seven, and my most grand gift, a bicycle, didn't arrive until just a year earlier. So make-believe, by myself, was the entertainment of choice. And it was always better outdoors.

Make-believe was inhabited not by the people who actually lived in my world but by vague historical events and characters from the book of lavishly illustrated fairy tales. In my solitary games, vanquishing Turks mingled with tormenting Nazis, and I stranded both in the prickly bushes where their skin was torn to shreds and their eyes consumed by the fantastic insects I pushed around with sticks or the stinging bees I chased toward them (having not yet been bitten by one and thus having no fear). Sleeping Beauty slumbered in a green cave created by overarching shrubs, and princes flew over the treetops. My only live companions were the ants, for whom I built forts made of stones and planted gardens of decapitated flowers. The ants were intransigent, but with the aid of water, shovel, and endless time, I managed to sometimes bend their movements to my will.

The pansies were my friends. Being plants and immobile, they always did my bidding. They had faces, happy ones, with crinkly black eyes and furry lashes, and wide smiling mouths in an upside-down heart shape. Best of all, with their varieties of color and markings they were all different, like people, and could be turned into any imagined heroine or villain.

The world of the garden was an escape from the adults, who

pinched my cheeks, exclaimed over my height, and begged hugs and kisses. The incessant demand that I smile was frightening. As living proof that Hitler had failed, I was expected to be radiantly cheerful, a chubby package of pink cheeks and beribboned laughter. But I was thin, serious, and thoughtful, perhaps made so by the emotional husks with whom I lived, whose reliving of the horrors, in words and glances, in tormented faces, accompanied every moment of my childhood.

In the garden, they couldn't see me and I couldn't hear them. Insulated from the adult world and its endless narratives of suffering and death, I was safe in the shrubbery, my head bent to examine a seed head or over the demanding construction of a mud house for the pansypeople. In the garden, I learned how to make the outdoors my refuge, my claim on sanity, igniting a flame of pure and lasting love for the natural world.

When I was six, my mother spent a week in a hospital near Cluj. On Sunday, my father and I went to visit. I remember nothing about the bus ride, the hospital, my mother being ill, or any worries I might have had. I also don't remember how I sneaked away, leaving my father holding my mother's hand, nor their fading voices as I moved slowly from the open door, then quickly down the long hallway. What I remember is the fascinating world I discovered outside, as I wandered straight into the tall trees that surrounded the cleared area by the building.

Here suddenly was nature on a new scale, vastly larger and more intricate than our little garden or even the city park. The trees didn't follow the straight lines of the chestnuts on our sidewalk or the oaks along the *allée* in the park. Here, there were no paths to follow at all. I could walk anywhere, and I did, my steps muffled on the dark forest floor, hidden from the world.

A messy place, with towering trees whose branches began far above my head, with undergrowth that made walking difficult and getting lost easy. Ferns grew thick at the feet of the giants. I climbed over massive roots, upholstered with black-green moss. Wine-red berries grew in the few open patches, and, lost to the world of humans and their fears, I gorged on their winey sweetness. A branch with prongs at its end became a tool for digging under the layers of fallen leaves. There I saw a universe of earthworms and glossy black beetles. Vernal pools glimmered darkly and I stirred each one with muddy hands. The air shimmered with the colors of the trees.

I climbed toward a knoll and scrambled up to the topmost boulder. I could see an open field, where all was drenched in sun. I walked there and sat down and the tall grass bent over me, holding me in a feathery nest.

Later, back in the woods, I sat on a log and listened but heard no familiar sounds. The only reminder of the world was the wind in the treetops, which came from somewhere far and even more mysterious than this forest. My adored father, my mother sick in the hospital, the loving aunts and uncles, all were remote and unmissed. Alone but not lonely, and utterly unafraid. Thirsty, probably hungry, but unaware of either in this wild, seductive world. I was bewitched.

I must have been gone a very long time because by the time I was found by my father and some strange men, the sun had set. It wasn't until I had children of my own that I thought of what my father had endured the afternoon I discovered wilderness.

Except for my mother's influence, there was nothing in my upbringing or my family history that would explain my irrational craving to own land and live on a harsh hilltop surrounded by fields, forests, and mountains. My ancestors were neither farmers nor landed aristocrats. They were—at least for the two or three generations preceding mine, which is as far as my meager family history reaches—poor Eastern European Jews who earned their living as cobblers, tailors, or, if lucky, tavern keepers. My grandparents on both sides had ten to twelve children. They were poor by any standard, but my father's family wore shoes and underwear year-round. And all of them, every last one, lived in cities or moved to them as soon as they could. Those who lived in villages had no land nor did they aspire to any; their ambitions were to move up in the world, from village to city. A city dweller was superior to a country bumpkin on every social and economic scale.

To my parents, forests and open land held terrors far beyond a drop in social status. Auschwitz was in a remote countryside, and when my mother returned, an orphaned cadaver, it was to the city, where flowering trees and birds were nature enough. As an enslaved laborer, my father had nearly perished on winter marches through the scenic Carpathian Mountains. He survived what his brother didn't only because his craft as a tailor kept him indoors a good deal of the time. Scenery meant danger. Safety, such as there was, was to be found in cities. It was in the city that my parents met and where I was born. It was where they were able to live among other survivors.

But I, born and raised in a city, craved something else. The colors, the silence, the breadth of that afternoon in the forest lived in the recesses of my mind. I wore it like a hidden souvenir thumping reassuringly against my chest as I walked, and ate, and slept, and later in first grade, when I sat among forty seven-year-olds, more alone than I'd ever been.

In the meadow, too, I am alone more often than not, but never lonely. Not with the whole visible world stretching away for many miles in every direction as I plod toward the blackberries.

I don't find early blackberries but I discover a large patch of still-green wild blueberries that must have just colonized the shallow earth between rocky outcrops on the highest point on the hill. I am visualizing wild blueberries for breakfast, soon! But I am bothered by the dandelions that ring this exciting patch. How exactly am I supposed to view these weeds that twinkle at me so sunnily from everywhere?

Dandelions, I learn, are an astonishingly useful plant. Almost every part can be transformed into something beneficial, from salads to teas to wine. The greens are saturated with nutrients, including more vitamin C than tomatoes, and if I remember to pick them young, I add the leaves to salads or cook them like spinach. Dandelions have deep taproots, and taproots are good for the soil, opening it up to water and air. The root has medicinal uses and can be roasted and ground for a coffee substitute. The flowers make a reportedly excellent wine, which I'd be willing to make if Ted would remove every one of the green sepals that encircle the yellow blossom from every single flower, which he steadfastly refuses to do. I explain that these would make the wine bitter, but he's not swayed. I have tried the tea and it's not bad but not as good as, say, Japanese sencha. Even the white sticky sap that gets on your fingers when you break the stem is useful, having germicidal, insecticidal, and fungicidal properties. It's easy to understand why dandelions have been an important component of Chinese medicine for a thousand years. Lastly, dandelions are excellent for entertaining small children, as anyone with two hands can turn them into necklaces and crowns. Plus, it's one flower kids can pick by the handful without having anyone yell at them.

Then there's the wonderful name, which I like so much I threatened to give it to my firstborn. It's an English corruption of the French *dent de lion*, meaning "lion's tooth," an apt description of the tooth-like serrations on the plant's leaves. Its scientific name is *Taraxacum officinale*, with *officinale* referencing "pharmacy," in recognition of its medicinal properties.

Dandelions are classified as alien or non-native because they were brought here from somewhere else. Given my history, I bristle at these terms. Natives are preferred over non-natives, at least in the plant world. Mostly in the human world I live in too, unless someone comes from a high-status country and/or has the "right" accent, which includes almost all English accents except those from the Caribbean, and French accents. Light Nordic accents are also acceptable.

Dandelions don't have the right accent. Despite the fact that dandelions have clearly made themselves at home here, they are far from fully accepted. They were brought from Europe by homesick Pilgrims, and once the genie was out of the bottle they multiplied greatly. Of course, coming here from Europe and multiplying also applies to many Americans of European descent. Like dandelions, many plants brought here from other parts of the world multiply to the point that they become perceived as invasive weeds. That's because they have an unfair advantage over native species; an introduced species generally arrives in a new land without its predators, pests, and diseases in tow. Native species, however, have an extensive array of pests that have evolved with them and that like to eat or kill them.

But if asparagus turned up on its own in my garden, producing food and exotic airy fronds, or if carrots suddenly appeared, I'd be happy to eat their roots and even their leaves, which I turn into pesto. Yet asparagus and carrots were both brought to us from other parts of the world, from the Middle East and from Europe, respectively. They are clearly food and not weeds. We have to plant them and coddle them because they are not nearly as resilient, as powerful, or as pretty as dandelions.

I wander around the rocky hilltop, searching for more blueberries, walking faster as my thoughts turn cloudier. Maybe these native versus non-native labels are culturally based, and we attach them only to some plants, which we then feel justified in attacking with spade and poison. It's a matter of how we've been conditioned to regard some of the most tenacious, irrepressible, and often beautiful plants.

I am feeling virtuous, having arrived at this seemingly logical conclusion. But our lawn is not a true lawn, just a meadow that is cut regularly; and the dandelions in the fields are hidden by tall grass by the time they get leggy and their sunburst blooms turn into fluffballs. Dandelions lose their good looks as they age, yet children love blowing these fluffballs and watching the seeds travel, each on its own little parachute, an effective dispersal mechanism on an admirably adapted plant.

As I wend my way down to the rows of remaining apple trees, I notice that new trees have taken hold near them. No longer shaded by the overgrown fruit trees, the seeds that have been biding their time in the soil have burst forth in a riot of new growth. The young poplars are growing in large clumps by the dozen, their trunks thin and pale and their leaves small and intensely green. From a distance they are green mist, delicate as smoke. Up close, they are whippy with new life. Another species of trees has also sprung up, these singly, but each little upstart is already taking up a fair amount of space with its circular profile. They sport leaves that vaguely remind me of elongated maple leaves, and indeed, several guidebooks later I learn that they are boxelder, a species of maple, very cold hardy, and, despite being native, a prolific self-seeder, making it what? A weed? An invasive? It also attracts boxelder bugs, which enter homes in the fall, but our house is far from them. It's also called poison ivy tree because of its leaves' resemblance to that hated plant. And it's short-lived, about a sixty-year life span—but then so are we humans compared to any tree. All in all, it's not a valued tree, several rungs below the unremarkable poplars, themselves considered "trash" trees.

But I like the leaves of both trees, and the tall and thin poplars look good with the squat boxelders. Neither species is out to take over the meadow, keeping discreetly to the perimeter near the remaining apples. When those go, these new trees will form a new hedgerow, creating the good fences that make good neighbors. They surely represent an enormous savings in labor and money over having to buy, dig, plant, and water new trees. Still, poplars and boxelders are not considered desirable. Arborists, landscapers, gardeners, extension services—all of them hold boxelders in especially low regard. The Internet has multiple listings for a variety of chemicals that kill both these trees.

Walking up the hill I come to the circle of blue spruce I planted the first spring after we bought the land, when they were each a thin, single stem with a few needles. I held out little hope that something so insignificant would survive a single winter on the hilltop with its massive frigid winds. But I watered them through three seasons the first year, and now each is close to my height and girth, a mysterious blueish green with cones that gleam purple in spring. They are native to the Rockies, but they are clearly suited to the climate and the soil here and can take whatever nature dishes out. The Rockies are not Vermont, but both are in North America. Does that make them native to Vermont too, the two being in the same country? Or just appropriate?

It's a conundrum. To me, not to Ted—who knows far less about trees and doesn't bother learning more. They're trees, he says, they look nice, we can use them. And it's so much easier to leave them than cut them. Who cares what kind they are? I care, and I try making my case. It's not a strong case because he has better arguments. It's not an arboretum we have here, he says. Leave them, he says, and he's done.

I am not. I know it's more complex than that. Poplars, boxelders, and dandelions occupy my thoughts, in the house looking out through the walls of glass, and outside, wandering through the rapidly filling meadow. I have no answers, only questions, and the experts who write the books I consult stop at labels. I see the value of poplars, boxelders, and dandelions. And I harbor a slowly growing belief that they won't disappoint.

# 4
# WISDOM

Plants dominate every terrestrial environment, composing 99 percent of the biomass on earth. By comparison, humans comprise a negligible portion. If the tower of life were a huge office building, plants would be the main tenants, taking up dozens of floors. Humans would fit into a single retail shop (a trendy one, to be sure) on the ground floor.

Why is this supposedly lower life form so successful? More successful than Homo sapiens with our outsize brains? A brain that can imagine the future, write Shakespearean sonnets and compose Beethoven's Ninth, explore Mars and change Earth's climate?

The answer in one word: cooperation.

We've known for a number of years that trees communicate threats to each other through chemical signals. Now we are finding that deep underground, plants also collaborate with microorganisms. For example, corn plants are able to manufacture sugar in their roots thanks to a partnership with special microorganisms. But what they don't use, they send to nearby bean plants in return for the nitrogen bean plants send their way. Native Americans knew that corn, beans, and squash, the "three sisters," are best grown together because corn provides a stalk for the beans to climb on, squash provides shade and keeps moisture in, and beans feed the other two. But as we learn more about plant cooperation, we see that it goes well beyond the obvious.

"There are dozens of fungi and bacteria living inside a single maple leaf, a whole living community. A forest is made up of a set of relationships, not individuals," according to nature writer David George Haskell.

Even plants programmed to be looking out only for number one suppress their natural impulses. A lowly flower called sea rocket sprouts aggressive, nutrient-grabbing roots whenever it detects a stranger trying to grow nearby. But if it detects another sea rocket, it politely refrains itself.

I learned all this and more at a Northeast Organic Farming conference over a frigid February weekend. I drove home filled with renewed admiration for the intelligence of plants. Soon after, it was Town Meeting Day throughout Vermont. I left that meeting wishing we could be more like plants.

At the meeting, instead of cooperation, divisiveness ruled. Instead of allowing individual talents to benefit all, partisanship reigned. Instead of taking advantage of available resources, close-mindedness prevailed.

Sounds like a microcosm of our federal government? Of course. But it should be easier to work together in a small town and a small state where people must regularly deal with each other and more people know each other than I thought possible.

We know people can and do join hands, because we've seen it happen—most recently in 2009 during Hurricane Irene, which hit Vermont especially hard. Scores of stories have recounted the heroic pulling together of individuals and groups throughout the state.

I am keenly aware of how fortunate we are to be living in such a magnificent place. More importantly, I'm gratified to find that most people I meet are sincere, community minded, and caring individuals. At the same time, I am disappointed by the unexpected distrust and dysfunction that dominates some towns. Unexpected because it's so counter to the prevailing image of Vermont.

Town Meeting Day starts my gardening season, the much-anticipated time when I get to line up the seed catalogs. Navigating the pages of lush tomatoes and foot-long beans, I think about the wisdom wrapped in those tiny seeds. They know that cooperation leads to individual success; that every plant has something useful to contribute; that roots have great value, but only when used to nourish the whole plant; and that new species may have new improvements to add to the mix. Most importantly, that collaboration is the key to a flourishing future.

PS: I am very happy to report that our town's politics have seen huge improvements over the past few years. And also that there are signs in other towns that the torch is being passed from the old guard to a new crop of young candidates who don't consider multiple-generation residency in Vermont a requirement for office.

CLOVER

# 5 THE ADVANCE GUARD

*Perplexity is the beginning of knowledge.*
—KAHLIL GIBRAN, "Youth and Hope"

We think of spring as a prodigal burst of life, but there's as much dying as birthing going on.

In reaching for the future, newborn plants crowd out any hint of bare ground. The pockmarked earth that looked so dead in winter, that held so little promise, is lush with rapidly growing grasses and a changing palette of flowers. I walk the days away, lost in wonder at this regeneration, this green phoenix rising from the cut trees. I can't miss a day because too much happens, the plants are on steroids, they are born and grow and bloom too quickly.

And still, death stalks the meadow.

The marsh marigolds in the wet fringes have come and gone in just days. Violets have lost their tiny petals, and those that remain are curled onto themselves, ready to blow off in the slightest breeze, with the brush of fur or feather, or just the touch of the chitinous shell of an insect. Bluets, dandelions, buttercups, golden Alexander, and Solomon's seal have all completed their missions: they've produced blooms, they've been fertilized, and produced seeds extravagantly. There's nothing left for them to do but sit there as their leaves yellow and their stems wither. Only their roots will remain a life force ready to push a new plant forth the following spring.

Then there are the calamities, the regular ones and the once-a-century floods or freezes or golf-ball-size hail. Sitting pretty on top of a hill, our land is protected from floods and from most late freezes. As the warmer air rises, we stay just above the freezing point, while on the road a hundred feet below us frost reigns. But nothing protects us from hail, which, driven by wind, shreds leaves, tramples stems into the mud, beheads every flower.

We don't miss the dead. There's simply too much new life to consider.

Clover, smartweed, vetch, vervain, daisies. In white and purple, in singles and in clumps, in your face and in far-flung corners they embroider the meadow. The grass grows thick and long and glossy. It swishes in the winds, showing off its sinuous moves. The red-winged blackbirds have arrived, turning the meadow into a lively nursery with their harsh chattering and sparks of crimson and yellow.

We are busy all the time. I water the vegetable seedlings and give them an airing on warm days. Put out birdbaths and hummingbird feeders. Plant more lilies and hydrangea, spread wood chips and launch into weeding, trying to get a head start. But they're always well ahead of me.

Ted is staking the grapes he had planted the previous year. He planted only grapes, not the most obvious choice in cold Vermont. But his father grew grapes in their yard, and Ted has memories. Not so much of the grapes as of the crushing of the fruit, done the old-fashioned way, in a large trough, where as a young boy he got to smash them with his feet. The thrill of that mucking in the slippery fruit, the smashing, the dark grapes exploding, the juice running over his feet, his father nodding approvingly, these images remain intense. The work during the months that followed is vague in his mind, but the first tasting of the wine lives on his tongue. So he grows grapes, and since we don't know how to make good wine, I make grape syrup that we turn into grape soda.

When not minding the grapes, Ted whirls around the lawn on the shiny new tractor, then cuts a meandering path through the meadow, then another, and a third to connect the first two. We meet to drink cold water. Dinner is late every night, late enough to watch the sun sink behind the Adirondacks and the fireflies wake to pulse across the fields.

We live on top of a hill, in the middle of a meadow stretching away in all directions. We have big plans and confidence, because we are strong and healthy. We are learning to enjoy physical labor, even when hot, tired, and bothered. There is nothing to stop us. We are blessed and happy in our ignorance.

Meadows are today all the rage with landscape designers and home owners, billed as the wildlife-friendly alternative to lawns. Years later, through the pandemic spring, I join remote presentations on native meadows. I listen to the enthusiastic presenters extol meadows' virtues; their beneficence to our threatened bird and insect pollinators, their beauty, their historical relevance, and—although no one stated it directly—their naturalness, which goes hand in hand with ease. Just look at this flower-carpeted meadow that you need to cut just once a season. See how natural it looks, how fitting it is, even in a small suburban front yard. In a rural setting, it sets the heart singing!

Even before the arrival of European colonists, the Algonquians, Iroquois, and other Native Americans regularly cleared areas of forest to create meadows for game. After burning, meadows grew in place of trees, but it wouldn't have stayed that way. Natural succession meant that the disturbed area progressed from meadow to woody shrubs to pioneer trees and finally to mature forest. The Native people maintained the meadows through regular burning, harvesting, and cutting. The many animals that roamed freely also helped maintain them by eating the emergent shrubs and trees. Only in the Midwest, where prairies are the last stage in natural succession, are meadows stable and require no maintenance.

Our acres have been through various states of man-made

landscape since the forests were first cut, probably when Vermont was in the midst of the sheep craze that started in the 1830s. In 1809, a man named William Jarvis sent a flock of Spanish sheep to America and quickly altered the landscape and the economy of Vermont. The shipment of prized merino sheep eventually turned the state's subsistence farmers into wealthy ranchers, fed the new woolen mills, and deforested the landscape.

The Vermont Map Center website notes that our property was "not prime agricultural land" (although I grow enough vegetables to feed our many visitors through the summer and the two of us for most of the year). Our elderly neighbors, who have lived here all their lives and whose families once owned much of the surrounding land, remember it only as pasture until the orchard was planted. Even the small forest growing in one corner of our property is made up of young trees, the old ones having likely been harvested several times.

A trip to the town office to search through deeds confirmed our neighbors' memory, at least back to 1905, after which I lost the thread. Huge books of deeds showed that there had been many owners, along with multiple repossessions by banks for nonpayment of taxes. Apparently there was as little profit in pastureland and dairy cows back then as there is today.

In the 1970s, the one hundred fifty acres of pastures, of which our land constituted one parcel, were bought up by a local orchardist, who soon sold it to an investment company that likely used it as a tax shelter. The orchards were then bought by an individual for reasons unknown, and left untended for several decades. And that was what we found the first time we saw our future land.

So for well over a century, this soil had been either foraged by large animals or used to grow apple trees. All along, it was not allowed to evolve into what it was meant to be—a forest of maples, beech, oak, birch, and white pine. We are the first to let it become a meadow, a pasture without grazing animals. Also the first with no experience growing much of anything, certainly none with a meadow encompassing so many acres.

The invaders knew this and sent early emissaries. There, in gracefully curving wide paths from the driveway down the hill and all the way to the fence by the road, were some foreign-looking flowers. They had the leaves of the common mustard, but their blooms were yellow instead of white. I looked, smelled, then walked away. It's pretty, I thought, then thought no more.

It rained on and off over the next few days, a warm, windless, heavy rain. I love water in all its forms but have a visceral dislike of getting rained on, warm or not, so I stayed mostly indoors. Driving up and down the driveway, I noticed that there seemed to be more of the mystery flower, but it wasn't until the rain stopped for good and I walked out to see, mud sucking at my boots—ugly rubber boots I've seen farmers wear, I thought with satisfaction—that I saw it.

What used to be green fields with pinpoints of color was now divided into swaths of yellow and green. A bright, cheerful yellow, to be sure. But . . . but a meadow is not supposed to be yellow!

I rushed inside carrying a few of the invaders. Ted was pouring himself iced tea. He looked at my hands full of plants, at my white knuckles, and said nothing. He slunk outside with his tea and moved to where I couldn't see him. He had already learned the signs. I pulled out the three books that should have helped identify the interloper. It wasn't until the third and most complicated volume that I discovered the enemy: the invasive mustard, yellow, of the charlock variety, but a mustard nevertheless.

In the weed "gallery" I learned that *Sinapis arvensis*, aka field mustard, wild mustard, or charlock, is of the genus *Sinapis* in the family Brassicaceae. It grows in North Africa, Asia, and Europe, in sun or shade, wet or dry soil. It is obscene in its seed production capacity, producing twenty thousand seeds per square foot, seeds that live for seven years and would be ready to germinate, grow, and overwhelm our meadow the following spring. It's allelopathic, which means it doesn't like to share, producing chemicals that inhibit the growth of other plants and of the mycorrhizal fungi that other plants need. It grows at an astounding rate, mutating within three weeks from a charming rosette into a tall, many-stemmed adult topped by a yellow inflorescence and multiple large seedpods. "A severe threat to natural areas because of its ability to quickly dominate the ground layer to the exclusion of native plants," according to the Vermont Department of Environmental Conservation. It may even threaten some butterfly species, and it appears to degrade habitat suitability for native birds, mammals, and amphibians. Oh, and it's edible, although wildlife and even insects won't eat it, which, I reason, clearly makes it a non-native. And now it's establishing itself here, moving into our soon-to-be magnificent meadow, rapidly reaching huge golden fingers into the green.

I rush out to share the bad news. I "reach out" in that irritating parlance, eager for Ted's concern, which should have in short order reached my own outrage.

"One year's seeding means seven years weeding," I shout out, a brilliant little ditty I made up on the spot.

He listens calmly, and when he speaks his voice is devoid of emotion.

"They look nice," is what he says.

"Are you serious?" I gasp. "Did you hear what I just said? They're *toxic* to other plants! Nothing, nothing will grow but that hideous yellow flower! Do you want yellow fields of mustard? Is that what you want?"

At this he seems to perk up a bit, but he's still miles from proper fury.

"Well . . ." he hesitates, then finally, "Let me know if you need help."

I don't bother to respond to the offer. The unknowing eye sees the superficial prettiness and misses the evil beneath. I fume all the way to the garage, thinking, that's men, whether it's women or weeds. I throw various murderous weapons into a pail and walk briskly to the nearest yellow swath.

I am prepared to wage serious battle. The muscles in my arms, weak from a winter of no gardening or swimming, are ready to be whipped into shape. My hands encased in work gloves, the previous week's rare manicure, indulged in for a wedding, already a distant memory. Manicures are for city folk, not for women trudging through damp fields in farmer boots. I keep my eyes on the yellow swath as I walk toward it.

The mustard turns out to be a pretty anemic enemy. I am almost disappointed to find that it pulls out without any fuss, the earth releasing the thin carrot-like taproot into my hands with a slight tug. There is none of the satisfying pop, none of the resistance and the triumph of victory that should accompany such a tall plant. On the other hand, the mere numbers present enough of a challenge. Huge piles build up behind me as I move down the hill. I look back at them often, and regularly walk back with enormous handfuls to pile on more so I can keep my handiwork in sight at all times. Those piles, even in their stillness, constitute a wildly cheering crowd.

By the third day, when half the contaminated swaths are still glowing in the sun even as the ones I cleared are beginning to radiate bright new pinpoints, I decide I've had enough. Ted had spent much of the previous day away from home, claiming that his presence was needed to train his new assistant, who I remembered had been previously trained but apparently needed a refresher course at a most inopportune time. He had rolled the window down and waved and thrown a kiss, then driven away briskly, leaving me to what he perceived as a task I perversely *chose* to take on.

This morning I am about to set him straight.

"You know," I start out reasonably. "This is not a choice."

"What's not a choice?" he asks.

I see he's determined to be obtuse. I invite him to come outside and take a walk with me. I point out the cleared swaths and the piles of the dead. Then I show the new ones that grew, budded and opened overnight, threatening to bury the green under a new blanket of lurid yellow. Finally we go inside and I show him photos of yellow fields with the mustards reaching unnatural heights and girths, unimpeded in their reach for complete dominion.

"This is what our meadow will look like if you don't drop everything now and join me in this battle," I wind up with a dramatic finale.

The not-fat lady has sung, and the argument that never was is over. He's getting into his outdoor gear and is out pulling mustards before I finish my coffee. Because now, *I* can sit and relax with a second cup.

I must admit that this mustard is not an ugly plant, nothing like the monstrous burdock whose taproot reaches into the earth's bowels, or the nettle that hides its sting behind coy baby-green foliage. But none of these form wide sweeps of color, being relatively few. From a distance, the mustard's ranks are not very different from any golden field of cultivated blooms or beloved wildflowers. If I remove my glasses, I can imagine that I am looking at a bright field of black-eyed Susan.

I put my glasses back on. I can't afford to let pretty interfere with the daily hatred I have to muster. The momentum has to be maintained. The mustard will soon be outranked by worse offenders that will show the mustard for the relatively benevolent enemy it is, one I will learn to ignore or eat. But for now, I am wrapped up in this single weed and its multiple thousands of minions.

I didn't always hate weeds. A long time ago, when we moved into our first house, I felt quite kindly toward whatever grew on our suburban lot. The first spring, when the lawn came up rather sparse, I was not at all averse to the cheerful dandelions that filled in the bare spots. Why, I wondered, did people go to such lengths to eradicate such a bright little flower? Why should a lawn be a uniform green when it could be starred with cheerful dandelions? It wasn't up to me to assign relative worth to any one plant. Dandelions and fescue had the same right to live and thrive. Surely, mine was a more sophisticated approach to gardening, a harbinger of the demise of the manicured suburban lawn and the rise of the suburban meadow, and I fancied myself a trendsetter of this eco-friendly ethos.

None of this happened, because well before the official start of summer, I stopped liking dandelions. The compact little plants had grown into leggy teens, waving on weak stems far above the grass, their tops large globes of white seeds, millions, billions of seeds equipped to rise with the slightest breeze and float to where more dandelions would grow. By the following spring, they had multiplied into a horde that threatened the existence of the ever-sparser lawn.

Over the following decades I became inured to the lure of wildness in a garden or a lawn, categorically rejecting egalitarianism. All plants are not created equal, and they don't have equal rights to reproduce. At least not in my garden, lawn, or meadow. Some species are sentenced to death, each and every blooming one of them.

I shudder at such statements. I am not a control freak. At least no more so than the average gardener, because let's face it: gardeners are all, to a greater or lesser degree, control freaks. We have to be, because we're at all times working against nature. We have a vision, and to reach it, we yank and pull and wrest living plants out of the ground. We move earth from here to there.

We thumb our noses at nature, watering our prized plantings while letting the rest turn yellow in drought. We prop up our lovely weaklings that wouldn't survive on their own. We feed our babies lovingly, spending on rare minerals and stinking fish emulsions. Each time I walk into the meadow or the garden and bend to pull a clover out of the asparagus bed, or a mustard from the clover in the field, I am controlling. Playing God.

But is clover a weed?

Most of our clovers are European imports, so not native. Yet the state flower of Vermont is . . . yes, red clover. That's because it used to be the leading hay crop in the Northeast due to its high percentage of nutritious protein.

Clover also fertilizes the soil. Its roots contain bacteria that combine nitrogen with hydrogen to form ammonia, and with oxygen to form nitrates, in a process called nitrogen fixation. Since the clover doesn't use all the ammonia and nitrates it manufactures, much of it is left in the soil for other plants to use. Plus, clover can provide amusement for children searching for the rare four-leaved one with magical powers. Despite its being an alien, clover has quantifiable positive properties as well as charm.

Here's the conundrum. In the meadow, clover is a valued ally. Plus it's pretty, and I happen to like it. In the garden it's a weed, but not an invasive one. It doesn't demand the world, just small bites of it.

Contrary to the popular definition of a weed as a plant in the wrong place, the clover in the garden is precisely in the right place—for the clover. And the mustard is in the most perfect place—for the mustard. Because weeds thrive best next to us humans, where they get pampered along with our chosen plants.

The mustard, however, was in the wrong place—for the meadow and therefore for me, who was tasked with mastery over the meadow. Is there a "right" place for mustard anywhere? In the meadow, it's a plundering invader with astounding reproductive prowess, the Genghis Khan of the natural world. (Genghis was famously prolific. Geneticists studying Y-chromosome data have found that nearly 8 percent of the men living in the region of the former Mongol empire carry Y chromosomes that are nearly identical. That translates to 0.5 percent of the male population in the world, or roughly sixteen million Genghis Khan descendants living today. These are the kinds of totally unrelated and utterly fascinating details you learn as you muddle through botanical information.)

As summer progressed, we spent days in the sun, yanking out mustards by the hundreds, by the thousands. We spread them out on the driveway. Drove over them muttering curses. Even peed on them, yes, urinated on them in the middle of the driveway. Repeatedly. This was done not for botanical reasons but as a final, irremediable insult. Finally left them to freeze over the winter. Having used up everything in our arsenal, the Vermont winter, we reasoned, will finish the job, as the Russian winter had defeated Napoleon's and Hitler's armies.

But we were dealing with a weed on steroids. Neither winter nor urine, not hideous curses nor the weight of cars killed it. By early April the following year, the undead hordes had covered the driveway with thick stems and bursting buds. The few that had escaped our focused weeding in the nearby fields had multiplied, forming new undulating mustard swaths amid the rich green. And emissaries of evil intent had been sent into far-flung areas.

There were many, many naysayers who, gazing at the golden fingers that reached into the farthest fields, insisted that ours was a futile effort.

"Impossible," they said. "Just look at how many there are!"

"You've really lost it up here on this lonely hill," noted a friend who felt close enough to give up being polite.

"They're biennial, you know, they'll lie dormant one year and reappear the next," warned another who fancied herself an expert because she was an outdoor educator. I could teach *her* a thing or two!

"Why not just leave them, they look pretty," suggested those who knew nothing about the malevolence that emanated from those bright bobbing heads.

"If you can't beat them, eat them!" was our daughter's solution. She claimed they were delicious, a cross between spinach and broccoli. But I was sure the depth of my antipathy would make digesting them impossible.

No one, not even Ted, understood that this was a war to the death. I could not lose. I would rather die of sunstroke than from the hatred that would surely consume me with curdling bitterness. The mustards and I could not inhabit the same hill. Either they or I would have to go. I was not going, because I was exactly where I had dreamed of being, living my own private fantasy. How many people are ever lucky enough to live their fantasy? I was staying.

The second year, we tried to enlist the neighbors. Not in helping us on our turf but in waging war on their own so their mustards wouldn't make new homes in our soon-to-be-mustard-free meadow. The elderly couple had seemed welcoming; we had visited them in their home, and they had been to our cabin, where they had sat in the uncomfortable kitchen chairs for an interminable time as we valiantly attempted to find common ground for conversation. So I felt confident this conversation would yield excellent results. Ted thought otherwise.

"They don't care like you do. They're used to just living with whatever comes. They don't have your energy. They won't even know what you're talking about," he argued. I found that thought impossible to entertain and asked that we at least try.

He joined me when we drove up their driveway and waited

in the car for the requisite five minutes, giving them a chance to ready for company.

After the neighborly pleasantries, I launch into the topic.

"We wanted to talk to you about the mustards in our fields."

"The mustards?" he asked, looking genuinely puzzled.

"You know, the yellow weeds growing everywhere. There, there, and there and there!" I pointed triumphantly through their window. As I suspected, their field looked much like ours.

They looked and looked and looked some more. And they said nothing. The silence weighed uncomfortably. I looked at Ted.

"Would you like to come outside for a minute?" he ventured. It wasn't the assistance I was looking for, but at least there was action as we all filed out.

I bent down and yanked out one of the offenders.

"This is the mustard I meant, but I'm sure you're familiar with it," I began, ready to launch into the grave consequences of ignoring them.

"It has a taproot," I pointed out. "So, if you let it just grow and grow, its root will continue to reach down into the earth until you won't be able to pull it out."

They nodded silently.

"And each of these little flowers, it's an inflorescence, you see, each of these flowers is actually made up of all these tiny flowers, so . . ." I continued, turning the flower head toward them, ". . . so each of these will turn into a seedpod, and each will hold about three dozen seeds, each of which will turn into a new plant. And each of these plants can make thousands of seeds!" I ended with a flourish.

I felt I'd made my case.

"The problem . . ." Ted began. "The problem is that these things travel, so they'll just move from your fields into ours, and from ours into yours, and into everyone's fields."

"And that's why we're pulling them all out," I concluded.

We waited. Another long silence.

"You're pulling these out?" he asked.

"All of them?" his wife echoed.

Another long pause followed our affirmative answer, after which he looked at her, shook his head and looked down at his boots.

"Well," he began, then allowed too much time to pass. "We just plan on cutting them all down when we brushhog. In a couple weeks."

"That'll take care of them weeds," she agreed.

There's a lot I wanted to explain. About the bobolinks and the redwings and their nests, and the eggs in the nests, and the embryos in those eggs, and these birds' shrinking habitat here and in their wintering grounds, and the perfect storm that's decimating them, and why we cannot, should not, ever brush-hog, at least not until the babies had fledged and realistically not until they all leave on their return flight.

But it was not my place. These are kind, decent people who are doing things the way they and the generations before them have always done them. We know nothing about their hardships and their thoughts, their history and their ideas. With our ridiculous worries about birds . . . birds for heaven's sake! We're as foreign and invasive as the weeds we're bothering them about.

So we returned to our mustard, to battle alone.

Ted was willing to "help," but it remained my project. He simply didn't share my intense loathing. A couple of hours a day was his limit for this activity, which consisted of moving very slowly in a stooped position in the hot sun while yanking each plant up by the roots, then walking handfuls to a pile of monsters. The piles were then moved to one central pile that grew into a small hill, which, seemingly dead, contained the seeds of a future surge. How to ensure that we really killed it constituted a future project. Would they end in fire or ice? Ice had failed; fire was next on the agenda.

Once, on a slow afterdinner walk in Palm Springs, California, where we were visiting friends, I rushed across the wide boulevard and stood transfixed, my fingers wrapped around the chain-link fence, my lips open in a silent scream. There, in an empty lot in this foreign climate grew clumps of golden mustard, the very same ones. They were stalking me! Showing up here, in the desert of all places, winking their yellow smile, torturing me! The friends watched me silently from across the road while Ted tried to explain, keeping his voice low. To their everlasting credit, they didn't question my behavior. At least not much.

Another spring. I gaze with joy at the grass growing wildly with the greening rains, the deep roots nourishing the regenerating surge. But I know better; it's simply too early for the outlaws.

The Mustard War has been dragging on for almost as long as the United States has been in the Middle East. The enemy has lost most of its momentum. Local pockets of resistance still pop up throughout the growing season, and in most of the original battlegrounds, but its numbers continue to shrink, and its vigor is far from what it was. In truth, so is mine. The mustard is not the enemy I thought it was. It's non-native and also invasive, but it gives up easily. These days, it takes just a few dozen yanks and the grass erases the memory of mustard. There will always be some skirmishes to be fought, but I am working on a victory flag that I will unfurl and fly from the rooftop.

As it turns out, I never get to fly the flag. Because as soon as we mostly rid the meadow of mustard, a new enemy surfaces innocently from the warming soil, one so abominable, indomitable, lethal, and devious that the mustard plummets to the bottom of the enemy list.

# 6 NAMES

Since my first walk in the fields that became our home ground, I have tried to know and name what I see. Years later, this naming of things, this taxonomic yearning, continues to drive me mad.

When I know a name, I can't always retrieve it. Often it pops out of my swampy memory bank days later. When I don't know it, but should, it's defeating. When I can't realistically be expected to know it, there's hope in the guidebooks and recently in the brilliant apps I downloaded to my very smart phone. But the quest still often ends in frustration. Because after a protracted search, when I finally zero in on the very plant—the one with the same rosette of leaves and furry stem, the flower with the same number of pale yellow petals blooming in the early spring—when I'm certain I'm finally deciphering the complexity of a plant . . . what do I find? That the plant grows only on mountain peaks or bogs or is a woodland ephemeral. Without any doubt, it cannot grow in this Vermont meadow.

Why this fixation, this mania of putting a name to every tree, shrub, grass, and flower that grows here? Does it make the greens greener? Or the golds more golden? Does knowing that this is a red maple and that a sugar maple matter? Must I have proof, with words and pictures, that the blueberries that magically covered the stony slope one spring are dwarf sweet? Or wait . . . are they low sweet? They are low and they taste sweet, and knowing what label botanists slapped on them will make them neither tall nor sour.

Yet people everywhere have tried to order the living world. And people everywhere see the same basic order, because beneath the great variety there are deep underlying principles. Psychologists have found that some brain-damaged patients are unable to order and name living things; it turns out all have suffered damage in the same part of the brain. So there must be a physical location where the ability to order and name the living world resides, making this drive a basic function of being human.

The names, too, intrigue me. Sassafras, for instance. An unremarkable tree in every way, neither imposing nor flowery, "Joe the Plumber" of the arboreal world.

But now take its name. Sassafras. A tart and spicy word on the tongue, a combination of exotic sounds. Does it not raise the status of this humdrum tree several notches? It lifts it right out of the abyss of tawdry commonness and makes it memorable.

Take another name, an ugly one. Burdock. It so perfectly fits this ungainly intruder with immense hairy leaves and roots that reach into neighboring states. Even when the name doesn't suit the plant at all, as in the case of vetch, an ugly name for a useful and delicate wildflower, I need to know its name. Sassafras, burdock, and vetch are the keys to simplifying this overwhelming green world.

No plants have as many aliases as weeds. Their names matter because how we name a problem decides how we approach it. If the weed is an invader from a foreign land, my first inclination is to eradicate it. Slash and dig it out. But we must know who's who because we can get easily distracted. Not all plants with "weed" in their name are invaders. Jewelweed is a native that supports bumblebees and hummingbirds and relieves the itch of poison ivy.

There's more.

One moment I see a plant one way, and the next time I see it differently. The two are the same plant, separated only by feet or hours. But the slant of light or the neighboring plants make them appear different. So we name the plant to know it when we see it, wherever it is.

I have learned a little. I proudly note that these young whips that have sprouted around the edges of the fields are poplars, not birches. Poplars, not aspens. This ability to detach a single tree from the green abundance is knowing the tree, and knowing the tree is integral to knowing this place.

Recognizing a plant among many others is like picking out a loved one from a hundred people walking away from a concert, knowing him by the tilt of the head, the swing of an arm. Yes, I nod. I know you. You with the velvety leaves stretching low, asking for my touch.

# 7 THE PARSNIP WARS

"Can't you get some help?" people would ask when we complained, which we did, at length and with gory details to anyone who would listen. Misery shared is misery reduced, although unburdening ourselves only seemed to replay the misery when we should have been relaxing.

"Four times we hired very buff young men," I would relate. "Each did great, working alongside us. We paid them handsomely, we sat at the picnic table with them to eat a fine lunch prepared with veggies straight from the garden. Then we sent them off with a six-pack."

"Good. And?"

"Each promised to be in touch, to come back, if not the next day, then the day after or the following week at the latest. They left smiling, waving from the car until we could no longer see them."

"And?"

"And we never heard from any of them ever again."

At the center of our complaints and the men's refusal to help stood hordes of poison parsnip.

It started out innocently. A tall, golden flower in a distant field. Not charlock, being so huge and exotic looking. I liked it and cut some to bring indoors to brighten the overcast day. By fall, that single plant had turned into a tight-knit throng, and I began to suspect we had a problem. By spring, I had learned

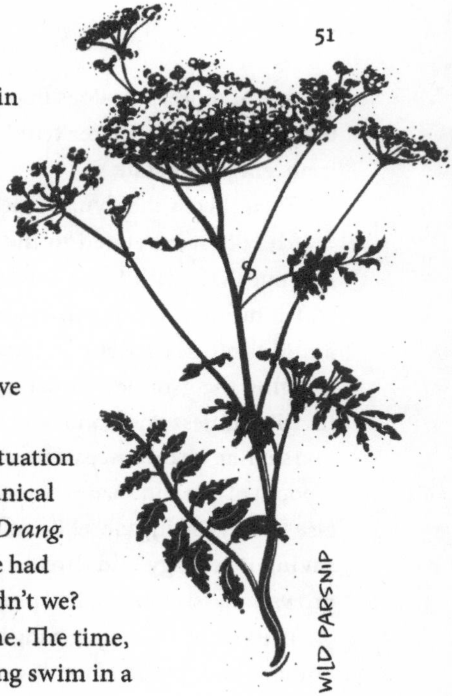


its name, and seeing it march in widening strips across the fields, I knew we were in for a protracted war. But it was hot and humid, and Ted showed no enthusiasm for yanking out tall weeds that he said were "pretty."

"Pretty? Pretty? Do you have any idea what they are?"

He didn't—not really—a situation I set out to remedy with a botanical tale bristling with *Sturm und Drang.*

Ted was not impressed. We had almost licked the mustard, hadn't we? We'd deal with this too. In time. The time, right then, was perfect for a long swim in a cool lake.

The first battles in the Parsnip Wars were tentative, unfocused. A big mistake, because by the following summer, the isolated bands had spawned multitudes. Shocked, realizing I had been sleeping on the watch, and with Ted now ready to join me, even while admitting no remorse, we moved into full combat mode, ready to use any outlandish method suggested and any yet to be invented.

By the second summer, finding that no truly effective weapon against this monstrous plant existed and none were in the offing, we turned ourselves into weapons. We became a Ted-and-Martha-machine of mindless demolition, a single fused organism of murder and mayhem.

Ted needed no convincing to join me in battle this time. Because this plant's evil is obvious to anyone with eyes, discerning or not.

First, there's the matter of size and girth. *Pastinaca sativa* averages four feet tall, but in rich soil and sun, it often grows to six feet or more, as it does in our fields. Its stout stalk reaches the girth of a young tree trunk but, perversely, resembles an innocent celery stalk.

Then there's the slyness, the trickery, the victimization.

The plant is related to the carrot and the garden parsnip, but that relationship is only a red herring. It's a biennial, which means it flowers in its second year. In the first year, it's a middling-size rosette of basal leaves, a bouquet modestly hugging the ground. Growing low among the tall grass, it's invisible unless one stands right above it. But all the while, it is marshaling its resources. Spread out, it receives the maximum amount of sun and shades out other plants, preventing anything else from growing close. By not flowering the first season, it's saving its energy and directing it down, far, far down, as it grows a massive multiple taproot that reaches to the bedrock.

In its second season, having built a formidable root system, it flowers. And here's a blooming example of its deviousness. How can I say this without perjuring myself? Yes, it's a handsome flower, huge, bold, gold, exotic. It looks like something that shouldn't be growing in a sober climate like ours but in some distant rainforest with thick strangling vines. Even its leaves are attractive, fernlike, pinnately compound with saw-toothed edges, resembling overgrown celery leaves.

But it doesn't end there. Poison is its first name because it is exactly that. It's related to poison hemlock, infamous for having killed Socrates, a not insignificant relative to have in one's family tree. While poison parsnip won't kill you, it will burn you, as it did poor ignorant me.

The plant becomes readily obvious when it reaches ridiculous heights and opens its small, five-petaled flowers arranged in an umbel of many small flowers, which combined measure up to six inches. And it reaches its glory during the hottest, longest days of July. You can see it then from great distances, nodding silently in the breeze, beckoning you closer, until reaching one, dressed in shorts and a tank top, you bend down and start yanking. Since its stem is hollow, it breaks when you pull, releasing a vile liquid that in the presence of sunlight feels like a flame has just scorched your exposed skin. You ignore it for a while because it doesn't make sense to feel such burning, until you feel it again, more powerfully this time, on the other arm, and when it finally reaches your cheek, you go inside to cool off and take a look. You see a red rash in multiple spots, and it scalds and burns, and even as you continue to stare, uncomprehending, it turns into a series of blisters.

If it feels like a burn and looks like a burn, it is a burn, you finally conclude.

Called phytophotodermatitis, the burn is caused by a chemical called psoralen in the parsnip's stalk and leaves. The brown discoloration that follows the blisters lasts for the rest of the summer and into fall. Forget about tank tops and shorts for the season.

Its seeds, while not poisonous, come in staggering numbers and are easily dispersed by wind and water. Furthermore, even while seemingly dead, the seeds are secretly living for as long as five years, during which time they can, under the right circumstances, grow and flourish. Since this is not a picky weed, the circumstances are always right. And since it's so adaptable, and powerful, and unstoppable, it forms dense stands that rapidly outcompete native plants. A summer drive anywhere, from New York City's suburbs to the Vermont-Canada border, features poison parsnip triumphantly lining highway medians, roadsides, and parking lots.

Oh yes, it is definitely not native, being descended from cultivated parsnip, imported from Europe, and gone feral.

So there we had it. A superweed. An invader that threatened to rapidly turn our life-giving meadow into an impassable wasteland useless to humans, animals, and, most tragically, to the bobolinks and red-winged blackbirds. How I wished it were only mustard, which now seemed positively benign!

And yet, as a vegetable, parsnip, which is native to Europe, was a popular food. Consumed in ancient Greece and Rome, it was much esteemed as an aphrodisiac. The Emperor Tiberius accepted part of the tribute payable to Rome by Germany in the form of parsnips. In Europe, the vegetable was used as a source of sugar before cane and beet sugars became available. It was introduced to North America simultaneously by the French colonists in Canada and the British in the Thirteen Colonies for use as a root vegetable, but in the mid-nineteenth century it was replaced as the main source of starch by the potato and consequently was less widely cultivated. Forlorn, abandoned, parsnip escaped from gardens to colonize vast areas throughout most of the United States and Canada. A case of evolution from a benign vegetable to a marauding monster. But who, in truth, could blame it? Humans hardly have a monopoly on ruthlessness and hunger for power.

But once poison parsnip threatened our meadow and its denizens, we had no choice but to organize ourselves and launch an all-out assault.

Caution was burned into my skin. No matter how hot and sunny and humid and windless the day, we went out each morning in full battle gear: socks pulled over long pants, long sleeves, high neckline, wide-brimmed hat, and heavy gloves. Standing outside the house, we surveyed the invasion and each chose a vaguely rectangular area for our day's attack, which we divided in two. For up to three hours, depending on the heat, tolerance to sweat, and the physical and emotional energy each was able to summon, we weeded. We were poked, tripped, bruised, scratched, and bloodied, our clothes a meager defense.

Weeding anything is like housecleaning. There's the dirt you see and the dirt you uncover as you clean. Here, there were the yellow heads we could spot from the house gazing down through the meadow, and the uncountable small ones you couldn't ignore once you bent down to yank a large plant. Thus the area we set aside for the day's work was never, ever completed.

We started out together but mostly worked alone. Sometimes we met at the corners of our rectangles, or walking to a common pile to deposit the pulled carcasses. Often we worked at opposite ends of the meadow.

It was best to work alone, because weeding some twenty acres of poison parsnip does not make for friendly conversation. It consists mostly of nonverbal communication, a blend of my whining and moaning and Ted's cursing in multiple languages, including some he doesn't speak. It's possible some are not languages at all, but I could tell they were curses by the not-so-subtle body language and the tone of voice. These were elicited by the worst offenders, the parsnips that had grown so massive that large implements were needed to pry the roots out of the ground. Also, and here's another example of parsnip's duplicity: the regular breaking off of the smallest ones in the middle of their weak root, which, left in the ground, would produce a new plant.

The best were the average-size plants. With the proper grip at ground level, these could be yanked out whole. Often the yank demanded so much energy that I landed on my backside with the trophy in the air, a tortured yell escaping. This meant I missed out on the satisfying whomp, the sound of relief, of emptiness, the grateful gasp of the earth yielding up the noxious root. And on the low crunch as the root is drawn up through the earth. With the stalk in the air, I also missed out on the satisfying weight of the soon-to-be-dead monster in my arms, its pliant drape, its heavy flowerhead already losing its vigor.

On a good day, when the ground was wet after rain, we could amass four hills of trophies, about a third of a truckload. After a week or two with no rain, each plant took three or four times longer. But we couldn't wait for rain. We were hostages of the parsnip's life cycle. Put it off, and it would turn to seed before we got to it, giving birth to who knew how many progeny.

That thought, and a fury I managed to build up on a daily basis, kept me going. Where did you come from, I ask, the voice in my head throbbing with rage. How dare you colonize our hill, the land I pledged to keep as a meadow for the elegant bobolinks with their drunken song? They must build their nests in the tall grass, lay their eggs, raise their young, and then fly a thousand miles to their wintering grounds, where they're poisoned by pesticides. This place is among their diminishing chances to live, to reproduce and return in spring, where I can walk the fields among them.

The immense loathing powered my muscles, strengthened my smothering hold on the stalks. If I stayed with it long enough, and if the endorphins kicked in, it built into a rapid rhythm. Bend, grab, yank, yank. Bend, grab, yank. Bend grab, yank, yank, yank. After the third unsuccessful yank, I would go for the digging fork. Ultimately, the furnace of the sky bearing down and my throbbing lower back became too much to ignore. I would walk the last armful to the nearest pile, shove the fork into the earth, and give up for the day. Ted would continue to work for a while after I limped to the house, but he, too, would soon be driven away by exhaustion.

We would then drive straight to "our" wilderness lake, where without preliminaries we'd walk up and over the boulders, fling off clothes, and wade straight into the glittering water.

There's nothing more calming than floating on a wilderness lake. All emotion dissolves. My ears in the warm water (yes, the water in a small lake in southern Vermont regularly reaches air temperatures at the height of summer), I'm plunged into a heavy silence. All I hear is my own breathing, which has lost its raggedness and is now even and slow. My eyes see into the depths of sky, penetrate the layers of cobalt air. I close them and let the soft ripples take me where they will.

Back on land, I'm struck by the unspoiled forest of fragrant cedars and tall pines, the ground a jumble of shrubs, thin grass, and stones. A solid deep-green world, with nary a weed in sight.

I love to be in it, but as far back as I remember I longed for a sun-drenched meadow under a huge bowl of sky. And for a while, I had it.

It was bound to happen. With so many sources and modes of transport, how could it not? Birds leave their seeded droppings everywhere. Animals carry seeds in their fur, and the meadow is home to hundreds of field mice, to voles and moles, chipmunks and snakes. Deer congregate by the apple trees along the hedgerow, crisscrossing the meadow on their way to other playgrounds.

Then there's the machinery, a wide brushhog mounted on an ancient tractor. That equipment has cut many fields over many years. As it moves noisily through our meadow, chopping down the tall grass, it spreads whatever was stuck to rubber and metal onto our receptive soil. But there's no choice. Forests are nature's default state around here. Once a year, the meadow must be cut.

We, too, do our share. I thought I was being environmentally correct when instead of buying compost in bags, I bought a truckload from a nearby farmer. Within a week, the rich dark pile was a flourishing green, studded with an endless array of familiar and unfamiliar weeds racing toward the sun, from ferns and horsetail to dandelion and dock. We covered the mound with black plastic to wait out the season as the hordes fried in the sun.

Most of the time, we don't even know that we contribute to the invasion, that we, too, have been recruited. On every walk through the meadow we carry seeds that lodge in our clothes and hair and the soles of our shoes.

By the end of the fourth summer, when the truckloads of parsnip carcasses had decreased from four to three, we realized that brute strength, which in any case was ebbing, would not suffice. We had to outsmart the parsnip. I would do more research, seek out more experts. The "Got Weeds" guy had visited us recently. He walked the meadow with us and saluted our accomplishments thus far. He appeared unintimidated by our challenge. He'd seen worse, he assured us. Much worse. He showed us impressive "before" and "after" photos. A schoolyard and a town green, I think. Also a picture of a huge collection of pulled parsnip in haystack style, a riff on Van Gogh. He mentioned that he also turns pulled parsnips into crop circles and long rows. But our parsnip piles were in fact much bigger than his. He couldn't help us unless he moved in with us and spent his working life weeding our meadow, together with our continuing labor.

We learned that pulling parsnips is in any case mostly wasted effort. (We shared this new wisdom with the Got Weeds man, but, for understandable reasons, he rejected the science.) Like many highly successful invasive weeds—both native and non-native—parsnip can regenerate from the tiniest rootlet that breaks off as the multi-pronged root is pulled or dug out. Possibly even from a root hair, which are infinite in number. At the rate we were progressing, it would take our lifetimes and maybe our children's too to bring the numbers down to a controllable level. New options had to be considered. Patience was demanded.

Which works for me. Despite being criticized for being impatient, as a gardener, I am a paragon of patience. Because as a gardener, you can't not be patient. Gardeners live in the future, whether it's the next season or the next five years or even in someone else's lifetime. They can never be content with the present. Gardeners must possess imagination, and be always striving for a better future. I'm sure Eugene O'Neill had gardeners in mind when he said "Those who pursue the merely attainable should be sentenced to get it."

So I weed and wait and learn and weed some more. The future will be one of a magnificent prairie of native grasses and wildflowers. So magnificent that it will set the soul singing along with the bobolinks.

Such a future can be attained only at great cost.

# 8

## WISDOM II

My garden never lives up to its imagined glory. Which is how it should be.

The sun pours unimpeded on every inch of my flower and vegetable garden. Anything could grow here, I thought when I first saw the land, a cornucopia of beauty and food. I could finally have the garden I had always craved. A Garden of Eden without trees, where I could play God.

The first summer I wandered around the fields, searching for the perfect spot. In the fall, Ted and I marked off a large free-form area visible from many windows. Hauling cars full of empty boxes, we covered the earth with cardboard, then piled on a thick layer of wood chips. Whatever grew underneath would die, giving us clean soil for planting.

But peeking underneath the cardboard in early spring, I saw the whole of creation thriving in the damp soil. The grass and Queen Anne's lace, the blackberries and clover, were pushing up powerful iridescent shoots. Far from defeated, the weeds were readying for when the cover turned to rich compost.

Understanding their tactics, we added a layer of newspaper and covered that with more wood chips. Spring passed with no planting. Summer came, and I spent it vigilantly destroying the recurring pockets of weeds that continued to push through the layers while also amending the soil, soil so heavy that wrestling the shovel from it was accompanied by loud sucking sounds from the saturated clay.

The following spring, I strung string between stakes and

tried to drop the vegetable seeds in straight rows. In the flower area, we planted the thin shrubs deeply, dug in the flower bulbs, tubers, and roots. Watered, mulched, and watered, all through that first dry June and July. And weeded ruthlessly.

The garden thrived in the filled spots and glared accusingly in the empty ones. If I squinted hard in a certain slant of afternoon light, I could see in it the imagined canvas of riotous color.

The following April, I stood in the gathering warmth surveying the winter-killed hibiscus, the daffodils casting yellow shards, the garlic reaching sturdy stems. By June, everything was in the ground again. In July, the flowers looked tall, self-confident, having survived the cold nights, the winds, the pounding rains. The vegetables were spilling over the sides, the tomatoes' pale skins stretched over juicy flesh, the beans hanging in purple streamers, the pumpkins rampant. By August, all I could do was watch the future unfold.

A good deal of the future was lost. The cucumbers' ends rotted away and they perished of sudden infant death syndrome. The skin on the most brilliant tomatoes burst without warning. The wind tore the blushing petals off the lilies. A monstrous burdock grew overnight and nearly strangled the sunflower seedlings.

I mourned each death. Then, within a day or a week, I accepted each loss.

Because I'm able to impose only so much order on only so much soil. Weeding and enriching, dropping seeds and planting roots, are, in the end, compromised attempts. Yes, I reap food and beauty. But my control ends where the ancient soil and the organisms living in it, the violent winds, the pounding rain, and the withering sun take over. Not to mention the deer, the voles, the rabbits, and the moles. Older, more powerful forces dominate. Fortunately, those forces temper the disappointments with their own abundance. The wild sea of grass holds as much beauty as the lilacs and lupine I cultivate with much effort.

So why garden?

For food and beauty. And because the effort is its own reward.

Due to some mule-headed stoicism, I like physical labor. I enjoy the feel of spent muscles, the thirst of throat and skin. Tired, I stop often to focus, slowly, on the near and the distant. On the swallows darting on the lawn, the craggy peak beyond the lake. The work imposes its measured rhythm on my impatient self, forcing me to look and listen.

Digging in the soil, I lose my repugnance to earthworms as big as young snakes, to iridescent beetles and all manner of creepy crawly life. This ground is common ground, host to multitudes, most of which I'll never see and can easily forget are sifting between my fingers.

In *The Hidden Half of Nature*, David Montgomery and Anne Biklé explore the complex life that lives in soil, turning life into death only to create more life out of death. Dead plants and animals are returned to the soil, where an astounding army of microscopic life breaks them down into soil, which in turn feeds more plants and animals. The lives we don't see far exceed in number the lives we are familiar with. Microbes—which include bacteria, viruses, fungi, protists, and archaea—are so tiny that it would take one hundred of them to span the period at the end of this sentence. But if you lined them up end to end, they would stretch one hundred million light-years. My mind goes numb trying to understand such figures.

While bacteria and especially viruses get a bad rap, most are not only benign but absolutely necessary, even to the earthworms that do the heavy lifting when it comes to creating organic matter. Earthworms each day suck in 30 percent of their body weight in the form of bits of leaves and other organic matter, break it down, then release it back into the soil in a form the microbes can use, which then feed the plants in a form plants can use. But inside the earthworms are the bacteria that do the actual breaking down of organic matter. Microbes, especially fungi and bacteria, don't need hosts to break down just about everything. Even rock can serve as food to these ancient life forms. The secret life underground feeds life above ground.

The soil between my fingers is swarming with life feeding, breeding, dying, and the creation of life from death. In fact, we owe our life on earth to these lowly life forms. I think of this as I reach deep to position a tomato plant.

I am then forced to think like a tomato. Would my roots know to splay out once they hit the clay? Would my baby leaves mind the wind that charges through every day? It will prevent mold but will be hard on me too. And just how much of my healthy foliage do I want removed so those pregnant ovaries grow into large globes?

I do all this thinking. In the end, I am left trusting that the sweat and empathy will trigger the alchemy between plant and soil and sun, and that the surrounding wildness will allow me the small victories.

Jean Giono writes in *The Man Who Planted Trees* that of the hundred thousand trees his hero planted, twenty thousand had sprouted. Of these, he still expected to lose about half to rodents and weather. There remained ten thousand oak trees to grow where none had grown before.

Not a bad return on investment. And an invaluable lesson in humility.

# 9 SPEAKING OF IMMORTALITY

I found my friend Victoria sitting on the sidewalk, facing her house, her face flushed with effort, hypodermic needle in hand. I stood some distance behind her, and in her single-minded focus on the needle and the goutweed in front of her, she was unaware of my presence. She stabbed the needle into the crotch of a stem, pulled it out, and, grunting, stabbed it into a neighboring stem. Then she scooted backward on her rear, repeating the stabbing, pulling and groaning on another stem.

"What on earth are you doing?" I finally called out.

Barely turning toward me, Victoria said that what she was doing should be clear to me, given my own obsession with weeds.

"Are you really doing what I think you're doing?"

"What do you think? And what choice do I have? Do you really think I'm enjoying this? Do you think I love sitting here and injecting poison into this horrible thing?"

As her voice rose to a pitch bordering on hysteria, I went to sit by her. The sidewalk was damp, cold, hard.

"How long have you been at this?"

"Oh, just since this morning and for a few hours yesterday."

I looked in the direction she was scooting and quickly calculated that at the rate of approximately four hours a day, she would be unlikely to finish before the first snow flies. But I kept quiet. Instead, I asked if I could help. Fortunately, there was no extra needle. I was free to return home and contemplate my own weedy meadow.

Victoria's determination is exemplary and by no means unique. I've read about others who after repeatedly failing to kill the living dead, resorted to the same method. The key is to not leave a single un-injected plant. Eternal death follows lethal injection.

Classified as an aggressive invader, goutweed was dispersed around the world as an ornamental, allowing it to spread wherever it was taken. The smallest piece of the rhizome it grows from left in the ground will quickly form a sturdy new plant. It forms a thick mat, and, once established, is difficult to eradicate. Plus, it prevents conifers and other trees from getting established.

Just a few short years before, I might have told Victoria that goutweed was a beautiful plant, tall, elegant, with toothed leaves and topped by white umbels. I admired it and picked it when I could, bringing home handfuls to place in vases. Luckily, its roots are not easily dislodged so I couldn't pull a few to plant in the meadow.

Once, ignorance was bliss.

Robin is a laid-back person, an erstwhile hippie who takes life as it comes. So when I asked about her relationship to weeds in her large vegetable garden where she grows most of her food, I was shocked.

"You want to know how much I hate them?"

She didn't wait for the answer.

"So much that I set the barn on fire trying to kill them!"

Turned out Robin was torching her weeds. Burning them with a handheld propane torch, which her local hardware store assured her is super easy to use and is healthier than using chemicals, she explained. Except when you actually try it.

I myself only got as close to a torch as a YouTube video. The noise this small implement generates is not unlike a small forest fire. Its flame looks large enough to start a conflagration, so it must be moved around rapidly, while the dry weeds continue to burn long after the torch has moved on.

I asked Robin how it happened.

"Well, it's really easy," she laughed. She can laugh about it now. "I got too close to the barn and didn't have water with me. You're supposed to douse the burn with water if it doesn't die out quickly. Who knew? I thought the longer I let it burn, the more dead it will be."

The barn survived thanks to a hose not too far away. But Robin now pulls weeds by hand.

"And I hate them even more!" she added.

The only people who can maintain equanimity in the face of invasive weeds are those who don't know them. In other words, people who pay no attention and certainly do not garden. Those who know weeds through close contact do not like them, and most hate them. The hatred is on a continuum, from mild distaste to all-out obsession. Some invasive weeds do of course cause havoc, but our intolerance may go deeper.

Humans and weeds have been locked in a symbiotic relationship for some ten thousand years, ever since the dawn of agriculture and well before we started moving plants around the globe and encouraging their expansion. Before that, as hunter gatherers, weeds were either good to eat or were to be ignored, sometimes assiduously avoided. Once humans began growing food, they became intimately acquainted with these previously ignored plants. Weeds—plentiful, accessible, familiar—became the first vegetables, continually improved and enhanced. Our first dyes and medicines were also derived from weeds. All the common plagues in our lawns, from ground ivy, plantain, and chickweed to dandelion, wood sorrel, and lamb's-quarters, have medicinal properties that humans have been using for thousands of years. Herbalists are still discovering new medicinal properties in weeds. Our common drugs, from aspirin to morphine, also come from wild plants. So does the aromatic cup of coffee that lets me continue writing this book during late afternoons when I'd rather take a nap.

Weeds are not parasites, because they can survive without us, but with us they truly thrive. They delight in cleared woods, farm fields, enriched garden soil, parking lots, waste spaces, solar farms, and roadsides. They often explode when moved to new ecosystems, leaving their diseases and pests behind. In short, they do best where we are present. And just as it's in our nature to take things personally, it's in weeds' nature to seek out intimacy with us. Weeds test our mettle, as my friend Sue learned early in her gardening career.

In the early seventies, Sue was living in Colesville, New Jersey. The house she was renting came with thirteen acres of overgrown farmland and a 1944 Willys jeep. Being young and naive, she picked out a sizable plot near the brook to clear for a garden. A neighbor brought over an ancient rototiller to give a hand but advised that she first remove the big clumps of multiflora rose.

"They were enormous. He was, I'm sure, thinking I'd just give up," Sue recalls.

She cut back the monstrous brush little by little with clippers, then tried to pull the roots out by hand. After much circling, grunting, and pulling, she started digging under the roots with a trowel. She dug and dug and dug. She went to sleep and dug more the next day. She was convinced a third day of digging would finally release the first shrub. She bought a bottle of wine to celebrate her imminent victory. But as late afternoon stretched into twilight, she knew the plant had won. She sat down among the murder implements to brood.

"It could have been loss of blood from all the scratches, but crouched there, I finally devised a crazy plan."

I want to hear this. We do not—yet—have multiflora rose in the meadow, but I know it's only biding its time.

"I got a chain from the back of the jeep and wove it among the roots of the shrub. Then I attached the chain to the back of the jeep. Slowly, I inched forward with the jeep."

Yes, and . . . ?

"Well, there was a lot of back-and-forth and I could hear the roots grunting, even above the noise of the jeep! And, and finally, that horrible bush released its hold. YES!"

Sue repeated this successful strategy four more times then went to her neighbor's house. He looked at her silently, then walked with her to the rototiller.

"It was the best garden I've ever had."

She moved soon after, and I didn't think there was any sense in pointing out that the multiflora rose most likely reared its lurid blooms within a couple of seasons.

Weeds coerce our attention. I know my weeds much better than I know the flowers and vegetables I raise so lovingly from seed to infancy and through maturity. I recognize a thistle from a much greater distance than a lily. I know a thistle in any season and at any stage of life, from the first leaves through senescence, but I may not immediately recognize a hibiscus without its outsize blooms.

Because of this intimacy, weeds raise our ire. Even laid-back, peaceful folk can become emotionally wrapped up in what they see as a battle between humans looking to grow food and beauty and weeds perversely bent on disrupting their plans.

"I am on nearly a daily basis dealing with two powerful adversaries from the plant world that threaten my flower beds and vegetable gardens with hostile takeover," Nick responded in writing to a fishing-for-information e-mail I posted on our community's list-serv. "This is the forty-eighth year in a row that I have had a vegetable garden," he continued. "Back in my hippie, back-to-the-land days, I should admit that the garden was more of an opportunity for mystical marijuana smoking than a means of survival.

"I find mint and bindweed to be the most annoying. I use a potato hook to extract the roots. Knowing that it takes only one inch of subterranean root to regenerate the monsters, I count on many return trips. Like many things, the only path to success demands an obsession with a daily plan of attack. This will lead to victory! (I was a conscientious objector during the war in Vietnam, but this is somehow different.)"

He recommends "piling the casualties on a brush pile, where, in the dead of winter, with a foot of snow on the ground, a blazing fire may rekindle one's resolve. Geneva Accord does not apply."

One of the many irritating aspects of weeds (to humans) is their unpredictability. Based on long experience, we expect that certain invasive weeds would, if left alone, do what they have always done: invade. So we expend huge effort to get rid of them before they have a chance to follow their destiny, only to find that we could have been lounging in a hammock with a bubbly instead.

Mary is a botanist. She spent over two decades at the Nature Conservancy in several states from Maryland to Vermont, pulling invasive species from forests with scores of volunteers. The goal was to keep it from outcompeting the native understory.

"We put all the pulled mustard into black trash bags and left them in the sun."

Why, I ask, but she doesn't know. Maybe because it just feels good. Knowing the weeds are roasting, dying a slow death. I get that, having meted out similar justice to our pulled mustards.

As far as Mary knows, the effort continues, but she has moved on to other jobs. The mustard moved with her.

"I was so vigilant about garlic mustard, so unable to let them be, that for ten years I actually weeded them out all along my road. I was determined to not let them invade the woods around our house," she reports.

For years? How many hours, weeks, months did that take? A lot, is the short answer. And then?

"Then I gave up."

The mustard is still growing along the road, but Mary studiously ignores it. And her woods are still mustard-free. Why, I ask. She doesn't know. No one seems to know all the ways of weeds.

But weeds, whether native or not, are neither evil nor perverse, nor are they out to frustrate our needs and desires. They are simply doing what any living thing does: insisting on living. And if they happen to find themselves far from their native lands, they will make the best of it, often ending up more successful than they were back home, where they had plenty of natural enemies that plagued them and inhibited runaway success. Who can blame them? We have done the same, over and over.

Humans play an outsize role in moving plants around the globe, but in fact plants don't need transportation help from us. They've been hitching rides on animals, on the wind, and on natural debris floating in oceans since the beginning of their existence. Since the dawn of global trading some five hundred years ago their pace of travel and reach have exploded. They hitch rides in the ballast of ships, on the clothes of sailors, in suitcases, hidden in the pages of books, in the fur and hooves of animals, in pant cuffs, even in agricultural seed bags. Still more are openly imported as ornamentals or, less often, as food that escapes and flourishes in our gardens, fields, and woods, as was the case with poison parsnip.

A contemporary instance of good intentions gone terribly awry is the story of hogweed in Russia. Hogweed is the monstrous cousin of poison parsnip, multiplying its nastiness by growing up to twice as tall and massive, to fourteen unimaginable feet. After World War II, Soviet agronomists, keen to reboot the country's agriculture, took a shine to the plant. Thinking its enormous biomass would make good food for livestock, they ordered the distribution of hogweed seeds throughout the country. Today, as farming shrinks and rural areas empty out, the hogweed population is expanding by 10 percent a year. At this rate, it will devour Russia long before kudzu, known as "the vine that ate the South," makes it out of the southern United States.

Until the nineteenth-century Romantics started swooning over every living plant, the hierarchy of plants was seen as mirroring human society, with its layers of status and privilege. Weeds were akin to trashy people while the pampered rose was the queen of the garden. One nineteenth-century garden writer compared wild plants to Aboriginal people or "savages," while the pampered hybrids were like civilized beings. Before that, it was believed that weeds were put on earth as a demonstration of God's canniness as a botanical engineer, and as "salutary scourges of human arrogance." The American Romantics, reflecting the American penchant for wildness and individuality, saw weeds as the work of nature, which was deemed superior to man's. This view persisted into the 1960s, when "weed" became a favorite pastime. In truth, the Romantics' beloved weeds were all from some other wilderness on some other continent, because there were few indigenous weeds before the Europeans arrived. Native Americans lived relatively lightly on the land, creating few habitats in which weeds could take hold. But "weeds followed in colonists' steps like a loyal dog, sprouting wherever they went."

Once established, there was no stopping them. They raced ahead of the pioneers moving west, so that by the time they arrived, dandelions, for example, were growing profusely. What the pioneers saw, and what we take as this continent's original "nature," was already vastly different from what it was before the Europeans arrived. And as they set to work burning, plowing, razing forests, and keeping livestock, the weeds thrived. Most successful were the European grasses, which quickly covered the open land that had been covered in forest. These non-native grasses had evolved with livestock grazing on them and had learned to grow sideways, to form mats, and to grow multiple shoots. The native grasses, used to being only lightly munched by deer, never had a chance against the herds of cows and sheep that munched them into oblivion.

I see the power of these European grasses in our meadow. Their roots form thick mats that reach a foot or more into the heavy clay, soil so dense that digging in it after a dry spell demands mechanical assistance or at least large male muscles. I've never seen a single blade under attack by insect or disease, or affected by spring deluges or by summer droughts. It's always a vibrant green, even following several light frosts. Because the grass is in the right place for me, I had not thought of it as a non-native invasive plant. And yet that is exactly what it is.

The grass is at home here, as are we. We, too, came from elsewhere and are putting down deep roots, taproots most likely, reaching through the topsoil down into the rigid clay, tunneling deeper every season, corkscrews turning slowly, barely perceptibly, determined to stay. Because we, too, can flourish here where we feel safe and at home.

# 10 GRATEFUL

I have lots to be grateful for, such as:

That there are no tumbleweeds in Vermont, tumbleweed being a plant that can germinate in thirty-six minutes!

That after a morning of pulling parsnips, I get to spend the afternoon floating in a wilderness lake.

That there is no yellow rattle in our meadow—yet.

That the meadow is dry, so there is no Japanese knotweed either.

That the horsetail plants that grow by the cabin are no longer sixty feet tall, as they used to be three hundred million years ago.

That I will most likely be gone before 2050, by which time up to one hundred new invasive plants will have moved north to Vermont.

That the growing season here is only about six months long, giving me another six months of rest from my weed obsessions.

That we host poison parsnip and not giant hogweed, another member of the family, which grows more than twice as tall, with five-foot leaves.

That I have a few friends and some (okay, two) family members who sympathize with my obsession.

# 11 Toxic Aliens Taking Over!

"Where are you from?"

This used to be a common question directed at me, less common as the accent of my first language faded over the decades. The answer is complicated.

"From Queens," I'd answer, knowing full well that I was not answering the question.

"No, I mean where are you from originally?" would come the follow-up.

"My first language was Hungarian," I'd add, knowing I still wasn't answering the question, only delaying the inevitable.

"So you're Hungarian."

"No, I was born in a part of Romania called Transylvania." Transylvania was a distraction that sometimes worked.

"So you're Romanian."

"Not really . . ." I'd respond lamely, trying to bring the exchange to an end, which always left the innocent inquirer puzzled and unnerved.

Maybe I'm being purposefully evasive, but there is no simple answer. And I do feel slightly irritated. This "where are you from" question has followed me through three continents, making me feel forever the foreigner, the stranger, the outsider.

I have lived in this country for six decades and been a naturalized citizen for most of that time. I got most of my education here, went through several careers, and raised three American children who are raising American children of their own. We have owned several houses over the years, paid taxes year after year, and never missed voting in an election. I think of myself as American for the simple reason that there is nothing else I can be.

I am neither Romanian nor Hungarian. Born in Transylvania into an ethnically Hungarian family, I didn't speak Romanian until I was dropped, entirely unprepared, into first grade at the age of seven. Two years later, we had left Romania for Israel and I forgot Romanian as quickly as I had learned it. I then struggled to become like the Israeli *sabras*, the native-born who were deemed tough on the outside and soft on the inside like the *sabra*, the fruit of the prickly pear cactus (which, interestingly, is native to Mexico and the southwestern United States). I failed, mostly due to the fact that we left Israel to come to the United States before I had a chance to learn enough. So I am clearly not Israeli.

Neither am I Hungarian, despite the fact that it was my first language. After we arrived in New York City, my father forbade my brother and me to speak Hungarian to him. (My mother was exempt from this edict.) This despite the fact that it was the only common language we all had. Instead, he struggled to learn a barely serviceable English as rapidly as his school-age children. Like all Hungarian and Transylvanian Jews, he had been horribly betrayed by a country and a people whom he had once seen himself as belonging to, a people who handed him and his family over to the Nazis to be exterminated. Understandably, his pain was greater than his reason. Hence, no Hungarian was to be spoken to him. So I am neither Hungarian nor Romanian nor Israeli. Strangely, the only place where I am seen as clearly American is when I travel to Israel or another foreign country. At home, I am a mysterious hybrid.

Being from another part of the world does not make me an alien, exotic, other; I, like other immigrants I know and the many I don't know, think we belong here as much as anyone born here. But "The Question," innocent enough and with no negative implications, nevertheless casts doubt on my belonging, my rightness, my claim to being American.

Strangely, I'm almost never asked the question in Vermont, which is orders of magnitude less diverse than New York City and its suburbs, where I lived and worked most of my adult life. Certainly "native" Vermonters see me as "other," a flatlander from New Jersey, because they stubbornly want to assume all of us hail from the Garden State (although I've never lived in New Jersey and have even refused to drive its convoluted highways for years now). Nevertheless, if you're not from Boston then you must be from New Jersey. Since a large percentage of Vermont's population is from somewhere else, for the first time in my life, I belong to the majority. And I am comfortable belonging.

"Where are you from?"

"Would you believe New Jersey?"

Vermont's plants used to mirror its people.

Thanks to the small state's varied climate zones, from the so-called Banana Belt where we live to the Northeast Kingdom, which enjoys only some 125 frost-free days, Vermont features a diversity of plant communities. Hiking up 4,240-foot Killington Mountain, I can in a couple of hours pass from the warm Vermont Valley, which is similar to the lowlands surrounding the Great Lakes, to an alpine environment where temperatures are on average a full twenty degrees cooler. Just a few miles west of our house toward the New York border, the Poultney River takes my kayak through forests of white pine and hemlock, interspersed with fens and forested swamps of red maple and tamarack, closer to the landscape I was used to hiking north of New York City. An early spring wildflower walk in this same area yields the same ephemeral beauties: trillium, bloodroot, marsh marigold, and my favorite—anemone.

But during the years we've lived in Vermont, I have watched

many new plants move in. These come from somewhere else, which makes them non-native at best and destructive of the native plants at worst. Every late summer the roads are lined with impressive colonies of poison parsnip, spilling over the highway dividers and wending around the edges of woodlands. Spotted knapweed blink their pretty purple heads in the nearby state park, which, like me, dedicates its fields to ground-nesting birds. Worst is the Japanese knotweed that each year gobbles up more of the forest edge at the end of our road where I like to walk.

Some of these have likely been here for a while, at least since Europeans arrived to cut down the forests for farms. But their inroads have spread and speeded up, a result of increased human movement, a warming climate, and the little development there is here. Like the rest of the world, Vermont has also become just a bit more diverse in its people, even though it remains the second-whitest state in the country. But it has become considerably more diverse in its flora. Unlike the origin of people, which can usually be guessed or shared, the origin of the non-native plants is harder to discern.

"Invasives both old and new have been spreading across the state," says Mark LaBarr, conservation program manager at Audubon Vermont. "But knotweed has been around for some time. It was here along the Huntington River when I first started this work more than twenty years ago."

Vermonters seem as accepting of plants as of people. Sure, there is some resentment; people whose roots here go back generations claim to know how things work and how they should continue to work unchanged forever. They know better than newcomers from New Jersey, even those with expertise in areas that could greatly benefit a small town. Or so the logic goes. But I have yet to hear the fear and loathing I feel toward poison parsnip from any Vermonters. Or toward Japanese knotweed, having seen it rampage across our New York suburb.

*In the summer of 2013, a lab technician in the suburbs of Birmingham, England, beat his wife to death with a perfume bottle before killing himself several days later. In the interim, Kenneth McRae outlined the way he understood his own unraveling in a suicide note. "I believe I was not an evil man until the balance of my mind was disturbed by the fact that there is a patch of Japanese knotweed which has been growing over our boundary fence on the Rowley Regis Golf Course," he wrote. "It has proved impossible to stop, and has made our unmortgaged property unsaleable. . . . The worry of it migrating onto our garden and subsequently undermining the structure over the next few years, with consequent legal battles which we won't win, has led to my growing madness."*

On one of my walks down the road late in the season, I try not to stare at the knotweed in full bloom. Its flowers, creamy white, don't grow at the top of stems like most other flowers; instead, they form clustered spikes along the tops of the branches. It is a robust, bamboo-like perennial that spreads by long creeping rhizomes to form dense thickets. Originally imported as an ornamental screen or hedge plant, Japanese knotweed is native to Asia. I actually snip off some of the flowers, unable to pass up their exotic attraction. At the same time, I determine to speak to the landowners.

On a weekend afternoon, instead of doing my usual walk, I drive the half mile to the house. Pulling into the driveway, I sit in the car with the engine off, waiting for someone to come outside. This, I learned the hard way, is good manners in Vermont. You do not ring a bell because there isn't one, and you do not knock on the door or walk around the side to see if the residents are sitting in the back. You sit and wait until someone comes out to greet you. You know they're home because you see the familiar cars in the driveway.

When the man comes to the door, it's time for me to show myself. He knows who I am even though we haven't talked before. We chat about the weather, which in Vermont, where five minutes can turn spring into winter and back again, always lends itself to a lively conversation. In March, it's possible to experience at least two seasons in on the same day. The mud that sucks at your boots in the morning crunches underfoot in the evening. When done with the weather, he invites me to sit on the porch, which is the apex of neighborliness around here. Finally it's time to launch into the real reason for my visit.

"You might have seen me walk past here. Pretty often," I begin. "I usually turn the corner to go up the trail, the one for horses and snowmobiles."

He nods, which I take as a yes.

Looking down the hill toward the bend in the road, I ask, "Have you noticed the Japanese knotweed growing around that corner on your property?"

His face is blank, which is my prompt to provide details on the plant's appearance through various seasons, a brief history, and warnings about its insidious habits.

My neighbor's expression remains polite but impassive. I need to know whether he's aware of the expanding hedge of knotweed I am referring to. He assures me he does.

"I haven't heard about this from anyone else," he finally offers.

I am ready. Having managed a whole communications department, I come prepared. I hand him the red folder I had been waving about to emphasize my points as I talked.

"You can read all about it here. Then maybe we can talk again. My number is here, in the corner."

I am trying hard not to pressure, to stay away from what my children call my "Manhattan mode." The next move would have to come from him. He would read about this botanical horror that is colonizing his property and call me, I am sure.

He never calls. Sometimes, when I walk by the house, we

wave to each other distantly, but even these encounters are rare. Vermonters are fierce about their privacy.

It seems invasive weeds are more upsetting to me than to my neighbors or to the professionals at the environmental organizations I contact. Which is unwarranted, given that I am the one who is neither clearly native nor foreign, the almost stranger so difficult to fit in a box. We like boxes because they make the complex less so by setting up clear boundaries of who and what belongs where. Americans here, legal immigrants there, foreigners from Europe—legal or not—here, migrants there, illegals way over there. Invasives bad, cultivars good, natives best.

Is this xenophobic or just logical, based on scientific observation? Scientists fall into both camps as well as in between. The jury is out, but, as history demonstrates, attitudes toward plants can devolve into similar classifications of people.

The conservation movement started in the United States with Teddy Roosevelt and his circle of privileged men. They launched the national park system, forests, game refuges, and other public lands, the whole system of environmental stewardship and public access that has been called "America's best idea." These early environmentalists believed that a country's treatment of its land and wildlife is a measure of its character. One of the movement's key members was Madison Grant.

"Now that natural selection had given way to humanity's complete mastery of the globe," Grant wrote in 1909, his generation had "the responsibility of saying what forms of life shall be preserved."

Grant has been mostly written out of the history of environmentalism because his beliefs ranged well into racism, as I learned from Jonathan Spiro, a historian and past president of Castleton University in Vermont.

Spiro's book *Defending the Master Race: Conservation, Eugenics, and the Legacy of Madison Grant* was the culmination of his PhD thesis. It began with his shocking discovery that Grant enjoyed much greater admiration in Germany than in his native country. So great was Grant's reach that Hitler wrote him an admiring letter in which he referred to his book as "my Bible." Spiro became fascinated with Grant because he "wanted to understand how you could be both a devoted conservationist and a committed racist."

Grant was a lawyer, writer, zoologist, conservationist, big-game hunter, and friend of Theodore Roosevelt and other powerful men. He worked side by side with Roosevelt on many important conservation projects, and Grant himself went on to found the Bronx Zoo and preserve the California redwoods. What he's best known for, however, is launching the eugenics movement. At the end of the nineteenth century, wealthy big-game hunters such as Grant, Madison, and Roosevelt began to notice that wildlife was in steep decline, a result of over-hunting and the expansion of urban civilization. Alarmed, they looked for ways to conserve these resources for future hunters like themselves.

One of their favorite prey—the bison—had declined from millions to just six hundred animals. Grant saved the bison from extinction by creating wildlife preserves. He was successful to the point that something had to be done to keep the bison numbers at a manageable level. Culling the sick, separating the males from the females, and castration were employed, again, successfully. And thus was born the science of wildlife management.

It was only a short step from managing wild animals to managing the human gene pool. Conservationists, and the preservationists who followed them, were mostly interested in the apex species: bison, golden eagle, redwoods, and, among humans, the blond-haired, blue-eyed Nordic race. Spiro explained that the sterilization of thousands and laws forbidding marriage between whites and anyone who was not 100 percent white was how in the 1920s "wildlife management was applied to humanity and called the 'science' of eugenics."

Eugenics also had a great impact on immigration. As the "science" took hold, so did fear that waves of Catholic and Jewish immigrants from Eastern Europe, and even more so from China, would "taint" the Nordic race. The result was the quota system on immigration imposed in 1924 on "inferior races," including Italians, Jews, and immigrants from the Balkans and Eastern Europe, while immigrants from northern Europe were encouraged. The quotas remained in place until the late 1950s.

Eugenics resonated with the Nazis in Germany. Many of them were germophobes obsessed with purity who rejected tobacco, meat, and sometimes even sex. (Spiro told me Hitler himself was a strict vegetarian who couldn't stand the sight of blood!) This obsession extended to people who were seen as impure, as well as to the German landscape, particularly its dark forests of fairy-tale fame, forests that were seen as the crucible of the Master Race. Preserving these forests turned the Nazis into forward-looking conservationists.

The Reich Nature Conservation Law—the brainchild of Hermann Goering—touted the benefits of mixed-stand forests and selective cutting as opposed to the monoculture and periodic clear-cutting that were prevalent at the time. It also banned the use of exotic plants in German landscapes, "to cleanse the German landscape of unharmonious foreign substance." German botanists made the analogy explicit in calling for the destruction of a type of jewelweed *Impatiens parviflora* (), which they deemed a foreign interloper: "As with the fight against Bolshevism, our entire Occidental culture is at stake, so with the fight against this Mongolian invader, an essential element of this culture, namely the beauty of our home forest, is at stake." Hitler quickly saw the logic of forest and wildlife management applied to humans, Spiro noted. In Nazi posters, Jews were depicted as viruses, as a universal plague, as polluters of German maidens. Labeling Jews as dangerous outsiders out to destroy the native population culminated in the Holocaust, he added.

As late as 2002, Pat Buchanan's bestseller *The Death of the West* predicted the collapse of Western civilization because of high immigrant fertility rates.

In a more recent example of xenophobia, Donald Trump referred to the COVID-19 pandemic as "the China Virus." Whether the invader is a plant or a virus, such terminology can fuel hostility that can, in turn, unleash a wave of violent xenophobia against innocent people.

Here are some recent examples from the media of the xenophobia that pervades attitudes toward non-native plants and sometimes people. In fact, out of context, it's often difficult to tell which is being referenced:

> "Invasion of the Alien Species"
>
> —*Wall Street Journal,* September 10–11, 2016

> Non-native, invasive terrestrial plants are one of the greatest threats to the health of Northeastern forests.
>
> —Vermontinvasives.org

> An invasive species is defined as a species that is
>
> 1. Non-native (or alien) to the ecosystem under consideration; and,
> 2. Whose introduction causes or is likely to cause economic or environmental harm or harm to human health.
>
> —USDA Forest Service website

> Democrats want to give all illegal aliens the right to vote, collect welfare and live off the hard work of real Americans . . .
>
> —letter to the Editor, *Rutland Herald,* August 18, 2020

> "The Real Aliens in Our Backyard"
>
> —*New York Times,* March 11, 2019

> "Stemming the Tide of Invading Species"
>
> —Jocelyn Kaiser, *Science,* no. 285, September 17, 1999

> You're a "migrant" when you're very poor; "immigrant" when you're not so poor; and "expat" when you're rich.
>
> —Laila Lalami, "Still Not One of the Family," *Wall Street Journal*, September 19, 2020

This last one applies to plants too. We don't want to believe that a beautiful plant that appears to belong in our ecosystem could be anything but benign. Which is why plant nurseries continue to sell and people continue to plant non-native, highly invasive plants such as burning bush, which looks much like its name, and sweet autumn clematis, with its innocent white flowers.

The vocabulary I came across in some of my readings in reference to non-native plants bordered on violent, with references to vagabonds, invaders, interlopers, rampage, and extermination among the memorable ones—the same ones that occupied my own mind in my early, naive days managing the meadow. But the more I read, the more uncomfortable I was becoming with the rhetoric, which mirrored the debate on human migrants. Many of the headlines did not specify whether the reference was to plants, animals, or humans. They implied that all came here to multiply, displace, diminish, take over, triumph. Even E. O. Wilson, one of my early environmental heroes, has said that "alien species are the stealth destroyers of the American environment."

Banu Subramaniam, a professor of women, gender, and sexuality studies at the University of Massachusetts Amherst, writes about the social and cultural aspects of science. She traces six parallels in the rhetoric surrounding foreign plants and foreign people. First is the parallel that aliens are "other." Second is the belief that aliens are taking over everything, and third is that they are expanding in numbers and strength. That they are virtually indestructible is the fourth parallel. Fifth, they reproduce aggressively, just as "foreigners" have been considered oversexualized and superfertile. Finally, foreigners do not return to their homelands; they are here to stay.

But I also read about the whole science of invasion biology as a discipline in the midst of an identity crisis, with its very name under attack. New voices argue that the basic premise is misguided, that if you go back far enough everything is invasive as well as alien. And that native plants grow where they do because of physical barriers and not because of any particular historical or political reasons or a particular "fitness." A plant's geographic origins are not ingrained in its biological being. An alien is simply a species that comes from somewhere else. Alien species are alien in name only. It seems we need to develop a new vocabulary that will let us see non-natives in a new light.

I am all for equality among people, and was therefore having an increasingly difficult time not extending that fairness to plants. I like the international aspect of equal people and equal plants, the melting away of borders, even continents. It's a small earth, and we humans have already spread out our Starbucks and McDonald's all over it, homogenizing it and greatly reducing the exoticism that once defined distant places. Why should we expect plants to stay in their historical homes, assigned to them by the vagaries of chance? Let them go where they will, or, mostly, where we ourselves take them. They may, in time, not only become good citizens but even contribute greatly to their adopted countries. Just look at how the United States has benefited from its immigrants, which includes everyone not already here in 1492. Take a look at Silicon Valley, at academia, at our doctors, our Nobel Prize winners. Yes, Nobelists. In 2016 every one of the American Nobelists was an immigrant.

So went the argument I was formulating while taking a sunset walk along our meandering paths. I was well along to convincing myself of the rightness, the fairness, of this evolved attitude. Actually, I was feeling proud of how much I had learned. Until I came upon a huge swath of Canada thistle that was overwhelming the grasses. It was too late in the day to do anything but stare and remember the common description of thistle as a "noxious weed" and clearly foreign, being Canadian. One flowering stem can produce forty thousand seeds, which can lie dormant for twenty years, making the plant superfertile. Once established, it's unstoppable because it multiplies through both seed dispersion and roots that extend in every direction, as much as twenty feet in a single season, rapidly growing into a dense, immovable mat. Pulling or tilling are useless because the tiniest root fragment grows into a new plant, rendering it virtually indestructible, and like other invasive non-natives, it has no enemies. Now, having found this verdant meadow, it clearly means to stay.

I couldn't think of any defense for Canada thistle. It was never going to fit in by growing demure and letting others live alongside it. It was set to move from illegal immigration to total takeover. And it was not contributing to the life of the meadow either. Not like the goldenrod, referred to as "aggressive" because it's native, although it's just as determined to turn all it can into fields of goldenrod. But goldenrod flowers sag with bees, and its stems harbor overwintering insects. Thistle, on the other hand, would quickly render the meadow unfit for the birds, and for the bees, butterflies, and the hundreds of other pollinators dancing their lives away on the breezes on our hill.

And yet, thistle most likely didn't bring itself here. It was brought here, just as Ted and I had been. Our influence has been positive, to the extent that we have not taken advantage of the system or engaged in criminal activities, and have contributed our labor, decades of taxes, and useful paid and lately volunteer work in the community. Every immigrant I personally know or know of has also been a boon to this country, whether they build our houses and pave our roads or staff our hospitals and win Nobel Prizes. There are exceptions, of course, likely many of them, given the sheer numbers involved, but exceptions don't define the norm.

Plants, however, are not people. It is entirely possible that law-abiding humans deserve equal opportunities to make a life here regardless of their countries of origin, but not all plants have that right. Not the poison parsnip! Not the marauding thistle!

# 12
# THISTLE

Toxic. Alien. Subversive. Invasive. Evil.

These are the words used to describe me. They are all wrong, wrong, wrong. Even my name is wrong. I did emigrate here, but from southeastern Europe and Asia. Canada was later, about the same time as I entered these United States.

There are more names, all ugly.

But I'm not ugly. I am what might be called ruggedly handsome. At least in my youth, when I'm short and my leaves splay out in a neat circle, a deep and healthy green. As I grow into adolescence, I get leggier until my thin profile reaches higher than the grass. That's when I grow my—if I may say so—distinctive and possibly elegant flowers, each a flaring burst of thin lavender petals.

I can barely hold myself up then, and struggle to keep away from the other thistles, because there are always so very many of us. And that precisely is my problem. But it's also my power, because I'm young, vital, full of energy, and nothing, absolutely nothing can stop me.

I do what all flowering plants do. Turn my flowers into seeds and let them go, just go wherever seeds go, close to me or as far as the wind will blow them or the birds and insects will take them. I am, as they say, superfertile! Each of my blooms produces some forty thousand seeds, enough to never worry about losing some. If birds eat them, even better, because one hand washes the other, if you know what I mean. My seeds feed the bird and the bird moves my seeds around to near and distant places where my children can start their own families, spreading ourselves into this vast, welcoming land. Although, I have to say, this open, sunny meadow is one of the best! I plan never to leave.

But I can grow my family right in place too, with or without seeds. If my flowers are cut off by that infernal machine? No problem. In bad years I don't even bother with flowers and seeds. Too much energy. I have something better: ROOTS!

I can send my roots out into new territory. I spread my tentacles as far as twenty feet in any direction, easily tunneling through sandy soil or ramming through clay. And wherever they find the tiniest open spot in the meadow, as small as a quarter, I grow a new shoot that forces its way out and up toward air and sun. And a new baby is born.

I am a powerhouse!

I have no secrets—you know all this, of course, and do all you can to destroy me.

You do what people do. I do what plants do.

Cut me down? My roots still live, and they are wild things I send on long forays. Cut my roots? Cells in my stem can become a root, or my root can become a cell! Yank me out? It don't work. Because you can't yank out all of me. My roots are thick but also thin in places, so you always leave a fragment or two. And you know what that means. A brand new me or several of me, grown in no time from each tiny fragment.

You hate this because you're jealous (even though I'm the one who is green, but not with envy). Cut off your little finger, or your little toe, so small it fits under the other toes. Does it grow back? Never. No need to mention the consequences of chopping off your head, as mine is every fall, just before I've had time to turn out my seeds. Even a lizard can grow its tail back, but you can't replace any of your parts.

There's more. You could die, next year, tomorrow, today, this very minute. Not to alarm you, but just think of the many ways you could die . . . killer viruses, black widow spiders, cancer, or a malfunction in any of your parts, which, need I remind you, you cannot replace. You're as badly put together as the dark clouds above me that are forever wafting away and returning in new shapes. You, however, just turn to dust.

I am plant! Watch me sprout, grow, multiply!

# 13 WHO WILL LIVE AND WHO WILL DIE?

*Who will live and who will die; who will die after a long life and who before his time; who by water and who by fire, who by sword and who by beast, who by famine and who by thirst, . . .*
—Jewish High Holiday prayer

I spend as much time in midsummer looking out the bedroom window as I do in midwinter. Because it's from that window that I can see the patchwork of intense color that I envisioned and that the flower garden is really, truly, magically becoming. The vegetables—carefully integrated into the perennials—are adding their own shape-shifting hues.

That's from the upstairs window. When I stand by the garden, I see lots happening that was not in the plans and now detracts from the carefully designed drifts of color I imagined.

While most perennials are well behaved, flourishing within their own allotted areas, others are bent on conquering all available space. The echinacea and the pinks, the giant phlox and even the iris and lilies are marching into others' territory. I don't mind if the Turk's-cap lilies, huge and adding an intense orange, marches on, but the quickly fading echinacea needs to be disciplined.

Among the vegetables, the few asparagus shoots I was told to leave to feed the roots have gone feral, growing multiple stems and reaching well above my head. The dill has seeded itself throughout the garden and each cilantro seedling has become a sizable shrub.

And these are the carefully planted, watered, coddled babies that I myself put there! Do I now dig out the iris shoots that are popping up in every open patch? Yank out the dill or let it bloom into golden orbs? Dill flowers are showy, smell delightful, and add flavor to pickles. I decide to let them be. They are herbs after all, not weeds.

Or are they weeds?

It's been said that weeds are plants out of place. Or according to Emerson, they are plants whose "virtues have not yet been discovered." Dandelions are classified as weeds; dill is an herb we grow. Both have useful qualities, including simply looking pretty. And pretty counts, otherwise why would we plant flowers at all? The dandelion, I decide, as I go to get a spade, can live in the grass; on the expanding echinacea I must enforce some basic rules. Planted or not, it's out of place.

The echinacea doesn't wish to be moved. My trusty spade, small, light, and effective, made especially for women, is rejected by the packed soil around the intertwined, spreading roots. I lift the spade and try another smaller plant that has only recently moved into that spot. Nothing doing. The digging fork is next. After a few attempts, I decide it's too unwieldy.

Water, plenty of it, will soften the earth. I stand with the hose for many minutes, making sure the water penetrates well into the roots, which seem to reach way farther down than this midsize plant warrants.

The rest of the hours are spent digging, deep and deeper, then reaching in to hunt for the ends of the roots, which invariably means digging deeper still. When done, dozens of echinacea lie on the ground, their blooms smiling up at me. Spent, I, too, want to lie on the ground but there's just enough room to sit. And when I sit, I notice that the Jerusalem artichoke is pushing up healthy stems right in front of me. A gift from a frenemy (who in her defense did mention that it spreads "some"), it is neither native to Jerusalem nor an artichoke, Jerusalem being a corruption of the Italian *girasole*, meaning turning to the sun, and the artichoke resulting from Samuel de Champlain's description of its taste. Its tubers are reputed to taste good; it's native; it's big, sunny, and robust. And it must be eviscerated. It spreads astonishingly through its roots, which means that the whole network must be destroyed, something I thought I accomplished two years before. But they keep popping up in far-flung areas of the garden. Removing them means uncovering the subterranean world where their innocent-looking white roots are once again forming new alliances.

They are as aggravating as the vetch that has also made itself at home in my garden, and whose spindly roots, which also form endless networks, break apart at the first tug, ensuring that I can never win out over vetch. Vetch, the first to move in from the meadow, has colonized my garden.

Unlike its ugly name, vetch is not an ugly plant. In the meadow, it blends into the rest of the wild growth and is mostly inconspicuous, except when its vivid purple blooms spike up the green. Furthermore, vetch is in the pea family, and a nitrogen fixer that fertilizes the soil. And here's a significant trait: vetch is native! And yet, in the garden, its weak stems sprawl and climb up the lilies and over the roses, while its slender roots expand into a world of vetch.

Why is vetch a welcome resident in the meadow but an infiltrator in the garden? What about the grass that encroaches remorselessly on ground that I devoted to the Gloriosa daisy? Are they good guys or bad guys? Where do they belong?

I think about the hours spent at my daughter's house in Portland, Oregon, weeding ivy. Ivy creeping up the trees, over the old cement wall, between the stones and into every corner in her carefully constructed "wild" flower and vegetable garden.

"Is this all ivy? Really?" I asked the first time I first saw it. A naive question, I soon realized.

"Right, and if you really want to help, start weeding," she responded, pulling a sharp trowel out of the collection of garden tools that covered the picnic table.

I continued to stare in disbelief. So much ivy, the same ivy that is grown as a houseplant back east, the patrician ivy that covers the walls of our most revered universities and makes them the "Ivies." And here was English ivy, with its aristocratic heritage, a hated noxious weed.

"Is this happening everywhere around here or just in your garden?" I asked.

"No, Mom, it picked me to invade, only me," came the answer, which I fully deserved, followed by a botany lesson on the plant's affinity to the wet and mild Northwest climate, and its nasty effects, which include climbing trees, choking off their light and air, and weighing them down to the point that they are felled by a storm.

I got to work, and for the next four days, pulled, yanked, cut, and dug with all the vigor I was not expending on poison parsnip.

So ivy joined dandelions, box elders, and poplars in the growing list of puzzles, plants that can be viewed as both good and bad, depending where they happen to grow. We like stories with easy-to-recognize good guys and bad guys, with clear demarcations between black and white.

The story of plants was turning out to be mostly gray.

That some plants get in our way has been understood since humans began farming and replaced the ancient stable landscapes with tilled, fertilized, sunny earth that invited everyone to join the party. It was not to be helped.

During all that time, weeds were just . . . weeds. There was no concept of weeds being native or alien until the eighteenth century and Carl Linnaeus, who introduced the standard classification system for plants and animals that we still use today. Linnaeus would have done well to stop at plant and animal classification, but later he decided to add humans to his *Systema naturae*, published in 1735. He was the first to include humans as part of the animal kingdom, a brave act at the time, when humans were viewed as unique and beyond classification in the natural world. Unfortunately, Linnaeus didn't stop there. He continued to classify people further, as he did other organisms. People were divided into four "varieties" that he labeled white, black, red, and tawny. These characteristics were strictly a variant based on geography. But as his next step, in his 1758 edition of *Systema naturae*, he expanded the classifications to include "behaviour," in which he ranked the four "varieties," with Europeans at the top and Africans at the bottom. Although Linnaeus never used the word "race" in his own writings, the hierarchy he created continues to be at the root of racism even today.

The terms "native" and "alien" as they apply to plants first appear in the writings of Hewett Cottrell Watson in the mid-nineteenth century. Watson noticed that unrecorded species were appearing in Britain. He defined native as "an aboriginal British species; there being little or no reason for supposing it to have been introduced by human agency." This is a definition we still use today, even though many plants arrived on foreign shores without human agency.

Interestingly, Watson didn't attach any value judgment to either kind of plant; natives were simply better suited to the local soil and climate. And he went as far as recognizing that long-established aliens were acceptable citizens. "Both these classes certainly now constitute a part of the British flora, with just as much claim as the descendants of Saxons or Normans have to be considered a part of the British nation," he wrote.

Darwin shattered this benevolent view of a perfect God-created nature with his revolutionary idea of natural selection. Natural selection dictated that the most fit plants would survive in an environment. Native plants happened to have ended up in a particular place because they were the ones that survived in that environment, not because they were a product of a created perfection. I would add that no collection of native plants could be perfectly chosen, since some dominate over others, becoming, in effect, native weeds, as our goldenrod are doing wherever the fields are not brushhogged. Furthermore, I wonder if natural selection means anything today, given that plants are no longer evolving in the kind of natural environment that Darwin observed—or what to him seemed like nature uncompromised by humans. (As I learned later, there is virtually no such place on earth.) Certainly, moving plants all around the globe is hardly natural.

Until the middle of the twentieth century, botanists viewed non-natives with some suspicion, being unsure of whether the plants caused environmental harm or were symptoms of human interference with ecosystems. Basically, not much professional attention was given to the subject. This relatively benevolent attitude changed with the publication in 1958 of *The Ecology of Invasion by Animals and Plants* by Charles Elton. The book launched the field of invasion biology, which grew slowly until the 1990s, when the journal *Invasion Biology* began publication and the field took off. The year 1999 saw the formation of a Federal Invasive Species Council charged with responding to alien species.

But except in agricultural land, there is little consensus among experts about how to deal with non-native invasive plants, or even about whether they should be dealt with at all.

In Northern California, a debate has been raging since the 1980s about a plan to clear-cut hundreds of thousands of non-native eucalyptus, Monterey pine, and acacia trees to encourage native oaks and bay trees. There is a faction of environmentalists who want to see many of the eucalyptus removed because they claim that the trees are a fire hazard close to homes, or because they are non-native and make poor habitat for native species, or both. Another faction of environmentalists disputes that the trees are more of a fire hazard than what might replace them. They insist eucalyptus make valuable habitat, sequester carbon, and provide shade, beauty, and recreation. Opponents are ready to lay waste to them with repeated treatments of massive amounts of herbicide.

This while many US states have non-native state flowers, from Arkansas's apple blossom and Indiana's peony to Ohio's carnation and New York's lilac. And, of course, Vermont's own red clover, native to Europe and western Asia. In the same vein, nearly a third of the states have the non-native honeybee as their state insect.

I was being forced to rethink my attitude. Maybe alien invasives—or non-native invasives, as I was coming to think of them—are a human construct. Does this mean that all plants are created equal and I have no right to kill some while tending lovingly to others? Is it up to me to decide who will live and who will die?

I made the mistake of sharing this newfound wisdom with Ted.

"That's a highly evolved attitude," he complimented me, adding that he will "back me up fully."

"What exactly does that mean?" I asked, suspicion rapidly replacing wisdom.

"Exactly what I said," he countered.

"Does that mean you'll stop weeding, or what?"

"Isn't that what you want?"

"No, that's not what I want. I want to have the meadow as a meadow, not a weed lot. You're twisting my words to suit your own wants."

"I am not! I'm just taking you at your word."

"Well . . . don't!"

Right. Because each time I went out to weed, which was most every day in spring and summer, supplanting writing, cooking, baking, and reading for pleasure, glancing longingly back at the lawn chair under the ash tree before moving on, the garden shot this theory to pieces. Pulling on gardening gloves, I would walk slowly around the perimeter, admiring the newly opened blooms and the ripening vegetables. And I would think, Do these glistening tomatoes, flushing their first rosy pink, have the same rights as the spindly thistle that has shot up unseen alongside it, masked by the tomato's leafiness? Do I really have to let the bindweed wrap itself around and over the Russian sunflowers until it smothers the giants that I wait and watch for all through the early summer months? That just cannot be. We'd have no food and no beauty. Equality might be well and good in a forest or even a meadow, but is clearly not acceptable in a flower or vegetable garden.

It's a cloudy, windy day, not a lake day, so after weeding we take a slow meditative walk on the circular path mowed into the meadow, a path we call the Horizon Trail. This area of the fields—or is it the meadow? I'm finding everything confusing, especially the erudite definitions that go like this: "Field is a land area free of woodland, cities, and towns; open country." "Meadow is a field or pasture." In my days as an English teacher I would have labeled that a fine example of circular reasoning. I find "meadow" more romantic, therefore we take a walk in the meadow.

This area of the meadow is relatively free of the monstrous poison parsnip, which has mostly retreated to the acres adjacent to the neighbor's horse pasture.

"Look up," Ted encourages me. "Don't look down. Enjoy the walk!"

Time to move from the particular to the general. Keeping my eyes away from the high grass and whatever else makes its home among it, I look instead toward the horizon where the sky meets the nearby low hills. This expanded view encourages an expansion of the mind, refocusing it farther and farther toward the craggy profiles of the Adirondacks in the west, the low-slung cutout of Birdseye in the east, and the town, the college, the lake, and the interstate in the north. It's a grand view, one I take complete credit for when visitors marvel at it.

But moles, voles, woodchucks, and chipmunks also use the path, digging big and small tunnels, so the path is uneven, forcing me to look down repeatedly. And then I see the incipient leaves of thistles and the tiny rosettes of parsnips. I force myself to look up again, all the way to the banks of clouds sliding into each other, and think about things other than my weeds.

I think of my friend Barry, who created a wildflower meadow on his nearby property.

It's an accomplishment that sends him soaring and plunges me into depths of envy. Like most men who get into working the land, which Barry has as a very hard-working gentleman farmer, he has acquired a collection of big machines. He used these to till and double till and triple till the soil and work in lots of organic material. Then he overseeded the rich, humusy earth with a custom-made mix of perennial and annual wildflowers. I first saw the meadow in its second season in late spring. A carpet of color that waved in the breeze like a vast flag. It exceeded anybody's fantasy. Barry walked into the field and I followed. When we reached the middle, he took a deep breath, smiled widely, tipped his head up to the sky, then turned in a slow circle to view the magnificence from every angle.

"*This* is what you do in a wildflower meadow," he enthused.

Ah, yes . . . I did the same. Why not?

After some enthusing of my own, I felt I could pose the dreaded question.

"What about weeds?"

"What about them?"

"Well, I already see a couple of goldenrod. What will you do when more goldenrod and then a whole army of other weeds invade this vision of perfection?"

"Weeds . . ." he mused, and I thought I got him, but he quickly recovered. "Weeds, schmeeds. Weeds are everywhere. We just have to deal with them, don't we?"

I wish I had his cavalier attitude, one that might not stand up to the realization that all his big machines are useless against the weeds in his meadow. That he will have to either start again from scratch or go after them one by one by one.

For as long as I can remember, I longed to visit the Amazon. To see the pristine wilderness, the astounding diversity of plants, birds, insects, and mammals, the teeming life at the heart of the continent, the vastness virtually untouched by human hands. In a dugout motorized canoe on the Rio Negro in Ecuador, I sat entranced, barely breathing for the three hours we glided toward our destination on the river's shore, silently observing the primeval forest on both sides. Once arrived at the Native-run resort, I rushed to join the first group heading into the forest, leaving Ted to retrieve our belongings.

The forest was like nothing I had ever seen. The towering multitude of trees, the matted, twisted greenness, the impenetrable darkness of it. It was not beautiful in the way a forest in the Rockies is in its golden autumn, or a New England forest in its baby green. It was forbidding, off-putting. But certainly not disappointing. The strangeness alone was enough to keep me excited for days.

The Native guide, though, was a disappointment. He knew the trails, impossibly narrow tunnels barely discernible even when walking on them. He took us up to the top of the viewing platform, where, as promised, we saw brilliant green parrots, which he pointed out with scientific accuracy: "Green parrots," he stated with confidence. He ignored the ocean of green below us, and on the return trip failed to name a single plant. Asked about a blue shrub—a true blue, deep blue, storm blue shrub!—he called it a . . . "blue bush."

Still, there I was, and I had a couple of books, which given the novelty of everything were of little help, but I bravely ventured forth and found the short forays into the forest primeval, dazzling, and not a little frightening.

Except, as I learned recently, the Amazon is not primeval. There is no primeval forest, jungle, desert, or any place on earth with the exception of the polar regions that has not been inhabited, molded, altered, and adapted to human needs. The deepest Amazon included.

Archaeologists are now discovering that humans have been inhabiting the Amazon for roughly thirteen thousand years and domesticating the plants there for at least eight thousand of those years.

"Recent archaeological studies . . . show that indigenous populations in the past were more numerous, more complex and had a greater impact on the largest and most biodiverse tropical forest in the world [than previously thought]," says José Iriarte of the University of Exeter.

One indication of extensive human habitation are the trees themselves. A research team sampled 1,170 scattered plots far from modern human inhabitants to identify more than sixteen thousand different species among some 390 billion individual plants. And so they noticed that despite the enormous diversity, over half the trees were made up of just 227 of those species. Furthermore, about twenty of these "hyperdominant" plants were domesticated species such as Brazil nut, Amazon tree grape, and ice cream bean tree. That was five times the number researchers expected if chance were the only factor. The conclusion? These trees are likely to have been domesticated by people living in the forest.

"Perhaps . . . the very biodiversity we want to preserve is not only due to thousands of years of natural evolution but also the result of the human footprint on them," Iriarte notes.

The same history of human impact on places considered untouched by human hands applies to other tropical areas, from the jungles in Africa to the rainforests in Southeast Asia. Researchers are uncovering large swaths that had at one time been cleared for agriculture and industries such as smelting, and remains of complex urban civilizations in West African forests. Until about fifteen hundred years ago, much of the Congo was clear of jungle. The world's rainforests and jungles—which I imagined to be the last "wild" places—are second- or maybe even third-growth, a lively mingling of the earlier plants that survived human development and those planted by humans.

Even the California that John Muir saw as pristine, untouched wilderness was a mirage, one I bemoaned on our backpacking trip because we met far too many other nature lovers. What Muir was really seeing when he admired the grand vistas of Yosemite and the gold and purple flowers carpeting the valleys were the fertile gardens of the Sierra Miwok and Valley Yokuts Native Americans, who for centuries pruned, burned, sowed, and harvested this vast garden. When elders were brought back years after their tribes had been removed and the landscape was no longer managed, they said the landscape was "unkempt."

So there is no true wilderness or primeval nature in any of the landscapes I have lived in or visited. Yet all these places were undeniably healthy, rich, magnificent. They were also wild to varying degrees, even after being repeatedly altered by humans. Wildness does not have to mean the total absence of human presence and agency. The will of the wild remains dormant in the land, oozing through the cracks and crevices, through the planted earth and pasture grass. Wildness is ready to regenerate repeatedly because it remembers what it once was.

Pennington Marchael, a landscape designer in the New York City area, told me a story about a wetland restoration job his company did. The goal was to remove the soil with the invasive plants and plant the newly virgin earth with original native plants.

"We removed up to ten feet of silt. After we removed it, we waited for spring to plant," he recounted.

But when spring came, they didn't need to plant anything. It turned out the seeds of the native plants, which had been waiting patiently for half a century or more in their tomb, saw their unexpected opportunity and took full advantage. The site bloomed with a horde of the original plants.

"We didn't have to plant a single plant," he said, still marveling at the magical time capsule that is a seed.

Of course, the power in a seed is less admirable when it belongs to a plant we'd rather not have.

Given the power of seeds and of whole ecosystems, perhaps we should stop worrying about maintaining what we think of as original landscapes, and just move on to being the gardeners we are, treating the earth as the human garden it has become. We can then try to align our needs and desires with the will of the wildness that remains in a symbiosis that enhances both.

Which is what I was trying to achieve in our meadow.

It was at this point in my reading that I was beginning to wonder about our meadow, the envisioned meadow, now a reality, that brought us to this dot on Earth and has kept us here through mud seasons and stick seasons, sodden springs and snowless winters. We don't take off to sunny climes when November locks us in its grip of unremitting gray days. We live here through April's ankle-deep mud, scraping it off our pant legs and car windows. We feed the birds and stare at their colors when January's thaw leaves the world a dirty sodden brown, and green is still in the distant future. And we work to improve our community in multiple ways. We can never be considered local in this state, which demands at least three generations of uninterrupted residence and possibly other requirements I know nothing about. Nevertheless, this is our home. We have made it so by our commitment to it, and belong here as much as folks whose history here is considerably longer.

Like us, the meadow is also a relative newcomer to this hill, as are the field mice that scurry in and out of the garage and the coyotes that howl just outside the window most nights. And especially the cats, like the feral one that prowled the fields laying waste to the birds I saw as ours. (Cats, both domestic and feral, are considered the biggest threat to birds.) Like us, these animals had all come from somewhere else. Nevertheless, the meadow was excellent habitat for them, for the birds that called it their summer home, and for the clouds of butterflies, moths, and hundreds of species of unknown insects that floated above the native and non-native plants, filling the air with the song and buzz of thousands. (Except in the spreading *native* goldenrod, which the bobolinks studiously avoid and maybe others do too, because it's relatively quiet there.) Standing in the meadow on a summer day is like hanging out in the Times Square of birds and insects, an immense, loud, chaotic center of life lived to the fullest at warp speed.

In addition to the much-needed habitat, there is the meadow's carbon storing power. All plants grab carbon dioxide from the atmosphere to use in photosynthesis, thereby decreasing the amount of carbon dioxide in our air. Forests, with their huge plants, clearly *capture* more than meadows, but uncut fields are more efficient at *storing* carbon because they use a different photosynthesis method.

Photosynthesis is the process by which plants capture energy from the sun to make carbohydrates. Some 85 percent of plants, including food crops and trees, carry out C3 photosynthesis. Meadows use a different photosynthesis pathway called C4. It turns out C4 is a more efficient type of photosynthesis because, unlike C3, it is not stopped by sunny, dry conditions. So meadow plants spend more time photosynthesizing. The more photosynthesis, the more carbon storage, which makes a flourishing meadow a very efficient carbon sink.

A meadow earns its keep. Most of the grasses and flowers—native or not—contribute to the benefits the whole ecosystem offers. Which is why I was having an increasingly tough time separating the good from the bad, the plant hosts that fed birds and bees from the non-native invasives that usurped the natives' historical habitat. History, as they say, is written by the victors, in this case the natives that were here before the Europeans arrived. But go back far enough, some two billion years, and every plant on earth that moved out of the ancient oceans onto the newly formed land was a non-native invasive, invading as it did a plant-free environment. Invasion is at the heart of all the evolutionary shifts over the course of earth's history. What I was seeing was only the latest manifestation of this altered habitat, which replaced many previous habitats over the eons.

The good-versus-evil metaphor confused me because the meadow refused to lend itself to black-and-white divisions. It was much messier, more dynamic, and more complex. It would take time, years actually, to unravel the strands and learn to accept most of the bad with the good.

# 14 LUPINES

From a great distance, we could see the fields, a shimmering purple. The color was shocking against the unbroken green of Iceland, the green of moss that upholstered every rock, that blanketed the mountains and bookended hundreds of waterfalls. What could all that purple be?

As we got closer, the solid color dissolved into individual pinpoints, which turned into flowers, hundreds, thousands of flowers, all of them wondrous, purple lupines. In Vermont, lupines grow in small scattered bunches on rocky slopes, but here they overlaid the valley. These elegant plants, with their palm-shaped leaves and tall flower spikes. We could walk in any direction for miles among the blooms. And I meant to do just that, fairly skipping out of the car and into the field, bent on this surreal experience in the purple sea.

Another car stopped behind ours. A middle-aged couple got out and waved to us. We waved back in a friendly kind of way. They motioned for us to come toward them. Were we not allowed to be here? There was no sign prohibiting anyone from wandering in. Also, we were careful not to trample the flowers.

The couple greeted us warmly and spoke in good Icelandic-accented English. We were happy to meet real Icelanders. The country has only some 330,000 of them to host more than a million tourists a year, so they're understandably not anxious to engage with folks like us.

"You know what these are?" she asked.

"Yes, lupines." I said, happy to remember their name. "Aren't they gorgeous?"

My enthusiasm was not reflected back.

"Ah, jah, nice, yes, but bad," said the man.

"Really? But why?"

"They are foreign," he answered. "They come here from we do not know where."

But are they a problem?

"Ah, yah, a big problem. As you can see here, we have so many, too many," he explained while waving his arm at the purple landscape.

I still didn't see the problem. What would be growing in the valley instead? The climate is too cold to grow anything other than moss. The little that's farmed, mostly pale tomatoes and small cucumbers, comes from greenhouses. So . . .

"Can you see? You can see, yes? It is too much. Like an army, a foreign army coming to us and not going away," he said, exasperated now.

I told him I understood and turned toward our car, a signal for them to leave. I whipped out my phone to write the day's haiku. (I recorded the trip in haiku, a quick and easy solution to boring travelogues.)

*Go sit in the field*
*of dazzling purple lupines.*
*Foreign invasion.*

# 15 STALKING THE EXPERTS

*Dear Expert:*
*I am working on a book for the University of Massachusetts Press on maintaining our Vermont meadow for ground-nesting birds. The goal is to keep the fields in a state that would be most beneficial to the birds. Currently the fields are being taken over by invasive plants such as poison parsnip, Canada thistle, and knapweed.*

*Would you be able to spend a bit of time with me to answer some questions I have on invasive plants in our meadow?*

*Thank you in advance.*

"You chose some real winners there," quipped Mark LaBarr, conservation program manager at Audubon Vermont.

Mark has been at his job for more than a quarter of a century, and he's seen it all. With all that experience and with his training as a conservation biologist, he zeroed in on the problem within minutes of our conversation.

"You know what your problem is?" he asked.

I knew it was a rhetorical question, and I've learned to keep quiet.

"You're seeing the transition from grasses to forbs."

"That's true, except the forbs, the flowers, they are . . ."

"Right, they're invasives. That's the world we live in now. But the transition is natural," he said, trying to reassure me.

"But what about the birds?" I asked.

"Bobolinks will deal with a certain percentage of forbs. They'll stay in a transition field. Then they'll move on, and you'll have brushland, and then you'll have brushland birds."

He said he loves to walk into overgrown fields and see half a dozen species of warblers.

We talked a bit about brushland or what Mark calls pollinator fields. Afterward I looked at pictures of such fields. They had grass and wildflowers, but these were dwarfed by shrubs and small trees. Brushland on its way to becoming forest. It looked nice enough, healthy, probably loved by all kinds of important insects and small animals, but to me not nearly as beautiful as our verdant meadow with its waves of tall grass.

I asked Ted how he felt about a hands-off approach. After just the briefest discussion, we were in complete agreement, a rare event. We do not want brushland. We want our grassy meadow.

I watch a recorded lecture by Larry Weaner, the guru of meadows. Why, he asks, was the Midwest not covered with forest like the East? I learn that the heavy soil, droughts, wind, and grazing bison kept trees from getting established. Also, that the Native Americans regularly burned the prairies to maintain the vegetation for bison.

Weaner warns against depending on lots of flowers in the first two years of a new meadow. These tend to die out, leaving empty spots for weeds to move in. A healthy functioning meadow is a long-term project. Match the plants to the site. Be patient. Beauty takes time to emerge. His meadows are breathtaking.

But we don't need to design and install a meadow; we're blessed with already having one.

Which is a good thing because the cost of installing thirty acres of meadow or even half that is beyond most people's means. According to Pennington Marchael, principal of Pennington Grey Landscaping, based north of New York City, the cost of planting a meadow runs to about six thousand an acre. Want lots of flowers? That costs considerably more. This doesn't include the maintenance contract for the first few years, which he wisely insists on with his clients. A meadow is a long-term investment, and he wants to ensure that the investment is ready to be handed over, he explains. Then his meadows can last indefinitely with an annual cutting and basic maintenance.

Before scattering a single seed, Pennington spends a year or more studying and readying the site. In addition to walking every foot, he uses drones to get a full view of the existing arrangement of species. There are microclimates as small as the shade cast by a tree, he explains, or the presence or absence of water, with adjacent sites being quite different from each other. Neighboring sites must also be studied, since they will inevitably have an impact. Once work is ready to begin, the site is cleared, then cleared again the following year. By the second year, there is a blank slate, ready to receive the necessary soil amendments and finally the seeds or plugs of small plants.

Then there is the investment in large equipment: an ATV with a spray rig; spray tanks, water tanks, and a truck to transport the ATV and sprayer; a tractor and a drill seeder; and a large truck to haul the trailer that hauls the tractor and seeder. The same thought kept recurring throughout these conversations: how great that we already have the meadow and all we need do is maintain it.

But *all* encompasses a lot in this case. Pennington says he is no lover of chemicals, but he makes a good case for using them.

First, because he insists that mowing, repeatedly, over several years, multiple times a season, simply doesn't kill the invasives. Based on the vigorous thistles that grow in the walks through the meadow that Ted has been cutting regularly for well over a decade, I have to agree with him. Pulling and digging? Ditto. It's simply not possible to get every last rootlet. Pennington cites a downside of mowing that had not occurred to me.

"Is it better to spend several years mowing weekly with a gas-powered machine, disturbing every life form?" he asks. "Or is it better to use a herbicide on individual plants once and let everything grow in peace?"

I have to agree that spot spraying the worst invaders is the better choice. The herbicides he uses and that we, too, use last only one to three weeks in the soil. A one-time light spray directly on the leaves is quickly absorbed by the roots, killing the plant forever. No additional treatments needed, no disturbing of nearby plants, no gasoline emissions, no crushing of nests or insects. Even if a whiff happens to end up on the grass it's fine because the chemical doesn't work on monocots, one of the two plant classifications to which grasses belong. The gallon of herbicide I bought five years ago is likely to last a few more years.

Bob Popp, the botanist at Vermont Fish and Wildlife, is another veteran, having spent thirty-one years at his job. He could retire tomorrow, he said, but why? He loves nothing more than being out in the woods, noting, investigating, leading field walks. He keeps track of rare and endangered plants in the state. The numbers are astounding: 153 state-protected endangered and threatened species, 480 rare species. Who would have imagined Vermont would have so many different plant species, over 2,800 of them? Most of these are flowering plants, but the number also includes conifers, ferns, grape ferns, clubmosses, horsetails, quillworts, spikemosses, and bryophytes, which include mosses, liverworts, and hornworts.

We're talking small, cold Vermont, not a lush rainforest, not even a temperate rainforest.

But Bob confirms what I had feared. There are many more invasives than there used to be back when he started his job, and their numbers continue to grow. He cited the usual causes: habitat loss and fragmentation, which create openings for invasives to move in.

"You should see the wind farms," Bob says. "They put in wide roads and the invasives thrive along these roads and into the surrounding previously unfragmented forest. It's very clear why they're there and not in the nearby unfragmented forest."

Then there is climate change, warmer temperatures encouraging plants, including invasives, to move north. This is especially noticeable in the Connecticut and Champlain Valleys, Vermont's banana belts, less noticeable in the state's Northeast Kingdom, whose climate is much harsher. But the climate is warming everywhere, and studies show that higher temperatures, especially when combined with elevated $CO_2$ levels, not only encourage invasives' growth but also vastly increase their resistance to herbicides, which is the weapon of choice at the moment because it's the most effective.

Bob has watched road crews cleaning out ditches, in the process moving seeds and underground stems or rhizomes all over. "Soon after they worked on my road, knotweed appeared along the ditch." He got to work immediately, and was able to eradicate the beginnings of what would have been a tragic spread.

So what do we do, specifically, about our meadow?

Thistle is an old invasive that doesn't take over, Bob assures me. I invite him to visit us in August, when parts of the fields are more lavender than green. Well, he admits, they do seem to do better in the clay soil prevalent in our area. The best control is prevention. In his own work, his goal is to "make the downward trend less steep." We could do the same.

"We have to choose our battles," he advises.

Wise advice. Which may work by focusing on the rarest, most threatened species, but in our case, the entire meadow was under existential threat.

"How do people think up these things?" wondered our friend Peter when I told him about Dr. Mike Kiernan, an emergency medicine physician in a nearby hospital who runs Bee the Change, a company he established with his wife, "the real gardener." Bee the Change creates pollinator fields under and around the panels in solar farms. The company is not for profit, and neither is there profit for the companies or individuals who hire him, but, as Mike explains, "Companies here are idealists, they want to do something about the climate crisis."

I am bounding after him as he moves between the rows of panels at one such farm, a relatively small one owned by a local construction company, and getting uncomfortable under the mask in the autumn sun. I learn that Mike loved bugs as a child and wanted to be a bug doctor. He soon learned to his lifelong disappointment that "there was no need" for even one bug doctor. Instead, he became a medical doctor while retaining his love for insects, especially the pollinating kind. As a premed student at Harvard, his classes were physically close to the Department of Entomology and its don, E. O. Wilson, arguably the world's leading entomologist. So in addition to learning about humans, he continued learning about bugs.

I, too, am learning from Mike. There are 275 native bee species in Vermont, 105 butterfly species, and hundreds more moth and bird species, all pollinators. It is for these minions that Mike covers the raw earth left after installation of the massive panels with a carefully calibrated selection of grass and flower seeds and plugs, all of them beloved by pollinators. He divides the area into zones, with alfalfa directly in front of the panel as a first cover crop, later interplanted with rudbeckia, daisies, and grasses. The area under the panels is planted with jewelweed, which flourishes in the dry, shady conditions. His goal is at least five species flourishing in a two-hundred-foot walk.

Today, Mike is unhappy. The area was mowed too early, not giving the plants time to set seed and multiply. But he cheers up when he discovers that mason bees have taken advantage of the special housing he designed for them. He's really excited about these bees, and for good reason. Mason bees, he explains, don't make honey but are extraordinary pollinators. Just 250 to 300 females can pollinate an entire acre of apples or cherries—and are often touted as being more efficient than honeybees.

What about invasive weeds, I ask. He stops to make a point.

"You have to distinguish between opportunists and invasives," he cautions.

I agree, but what about . . .

"I don't take on jobs in parsnip fields," he says.

Aha. So he, too, has his bad-guys boundaries.

JEWELWEED

If the area is not totally invaded, the parsnips are pulled by hand. And he's experimenting with a parsnip webworm, an age-old enemy of parsnip that's able to overcome the plant's chemical defenses. He asks that the tires of the brushhog be cleaned thoroughly to remove weed seeds from other fields. So do I, I mention, although who knows if it actually happens. Thistle? They're bad, he concedes. The answer is to mow, mow, mow, keep the area as a lawn, even if it compromises the pollinators for a while.

He, too, leaves me with excellent advice: "When you try to restore or change a habitat, you need to be modest. Very modest."

His words leave an echo that gains strength over time.

Mary Droege used to work for the Nature Conservancy in various states and currently teaches botany at Castleton University. One day she said something that turned my whole world of native meadow ambitions on its head.

"What makes you think," said she, "that your meadow is native?"

I stared at her, blindsided by this simple and obvious insight. Unaware of the havoc she had launched in my brain, she continued.

"Forest is native in Vermont and throughout much of the landscape of this country."

This conversation took place during the California fires of 2020, and she had that morning read about the fires that destroyed many of the beloved Joshua trees, trees that I had visited several times and never got enough of. The fact that they are not trees at all but yuccas, which are in the lily family, especially fascinated me.

Mary explained that non-native invasive grasses had made the desert more flammable, in an ecosystem historically not adapted to fire. Cattle brought into the area spread these grasses, while reducing the native grasses that they preferred to eat. Blackbrush, a native plant and very flammable, was also not liked by cattle. Which was good for the blackbrush and also for the Joshua trees, since blackbrush acts as a nursery for the trees by shading them and hiding them from rodents. The ecosystem was thus changed by the animals humans brought, from an open savanna with some big Joshua trees to a dense woodland that was now burning.

We agreed that our meadow would not burn, would be hard to set on fire even if we tried given its green wetness. This despite it's not being native. But I was still distraught. Mary tried to comfort me.

When she worked at the Nature Conservancy, they spent enormous resources battling bush honeysuckle, barberry, garlic mustard, and water chestnut, she said.

"But sometimes I wondered if pulling and digging out all these invasives creates more disturbance than just leaving things be. And are we going to do this forever? How? Everyone runs out of steam."

"We must work at the intersection of what *needs* to be done and what *can* be done."

Yes, sure, I get it.

Just as I was being handed all the logical pronouncements about the unsuitability of our meadow, the meadow itself was at its most stunning, a sea of billowing, lively green. So it was a relief to talk to Kevin Tolan, the grasslands outreach coordinator for the Vermont Center for Ecostudies. His job is to provide technical assistance to landowners and farmers on managing fields for birds and for hay, "striking a happy balance."

Kevin fell in love with grassland birds courtesy of professors Allan Strong at the University of Vermont (UVM) and Noah Perlut at the University of New England (UNE).

"It's amazing, isn't it, how they return to the same field year after year, within a couple of hundred meters, after their twelve-thousand-mile migration round trip?"

This is something that never ceases to awe him about bobolinks. As a student at UVM he worked for UNE's Bobolink Odyssey doing bird banding, and was thrilled to see that many returning birds were the same ones that flew to Argentina the previous fall. Kevin seems to love these birds at least as much as I do, so I feel safe sharing my distress.

"And yet," I start out cautiously, "several of your fellow scientists have been telling me that meadows are not native to Vermont. And, and . . . we should just stop fighting and let it become what it's meant to become. Brushland and then forest."

He agrees that meadows are not a major part of the endemic landscape here. Still, there were always some meadows, created by natural forces, fire, windstorms, and landslides. Native Americans also set fires, primarily in coastal New England, to encourage open meadows. Now we suppress fires and the trees are not high enough to create large clearings when they are felled by wind or landslides. So meadows are by now part of Vermont history. There was a period in the mid-1800s when sheep farming was the state's chief economic driver and the land was 80 percent open fields and only 20 percent forest, he reminds me. The numbers have since reversed, but the birds continue to return to what they continue to see as their summer home.

"Grassland birds are experiencing the sharpest decline among continental North American birds, so they need us. Their lives are intertwined with human land use," Kevin explains. I wonder how often he has to justify his life's work.

We talk about birds some more, leaving little time for figuring out just how to maintain the needed meadow. But no matter, he reinforces what others have said.

Cut the fields often, just mow them like a lawn, and be sure the machinery is washed thoroughly. Do it for a few years, while catching invasives early. There's no other choice, he says. The birds will find other fields in the meantime, and in time return to ours.

"Managing for invasives is the exact opposite of managing for birds," Kevin sums up.

Goats! Goats are the answer! They eat all the invasives but leave the grass alone. That has been the experience of Vermont Land Trust lead forester Pieter van Loon.

We don't have goats. Ah, but we can rent them. There are people who hire out goats for invasive control. Right, but we also don't have fencing to keep goats from coming and going at their pleasure. Well, that is a problem.

Pieter and I trade weed stories for a while. He commiserates with our challenges. Then he turns philosophical.

"What's native? Our human footprint is so extensive that trying to get back to what is natural may not be realistic."

I agree. In a few hundred years today's invasives will be the natives. By then, ecosystems around the whole earth may be indistinguishable from each other. But meanwhile, should we try to give the natives a fighting chance? Level the playing field a bit? Or just go with "Green is good enough?"

"I'm not willing to wait and see if the natives survive or not," Pieter decides.

I'm not either. Which means we have to find a solution that goes beyond trying to eradicate each and every invasive ourselves, trudging through chin-high grass through three seasons. EDRR. That's the answer. It stands for early detection, rapid response. Anything new that shows up in an established ecosystem is guilty until proven innocent beyond the shadow of a doubt. If it wasn't there before, it's almost guaranteed to be bad—a non-native invasive. (I can only hope this doesn't apply to people too.) I learn this at an informative webinar hosted by the Southeast Vermont Invasive Species Management Area. Unfortunately, it's too late for the sage advice. Early detection, yes. But no rapid response, beyond cutting some impressive poison parsnip flowers to enjoy inside. In my new informed hindsight, I never cease to be amazed at my former breathtaking ignorance.

A possible solution—actually two of them—arrive for a site visit on an unseasonably cold fall day.

Johan Desrochers and Timothy Brosnan are two young soil conservationists for the local office of the US Department of Agriculture, Natural Resources Conservation Service. Johan and I have been in contact for some months, so he's familiar with our meadow and its problem plants. Tim, who's been at the job longer, joins him on this field trip. The two may well be the best and possibly only solution. They will apply for financial assistance through a Farm Bill program that will pay for three-quarters of the cost of multiple cuttings a season and spot spraying the invasives. A similar grant had previously allowed us to have the apple trees cut. This project will be much more labor intensive and will continue over several years. They have reasonable hopes that if there are enough funds, our application will be approved.

By the time we all meet, I've stalked enough experts—including Johan himself—to have a plan to share. We talk as the four of us traverse the meadows, up and down, on cut paths and off, and all around the wedge-shaped property. Ted and I are proud of the way we keep up with these young men. Tim explains he likes "to wander," the favorite part of his job. Everything catches his attention, including a host of invasive shrubs I didn't know we had and a possible small multiflora rose that he says I need to watch in the spring. These discoveries, I figure, can only strengthen my argument.

But I don't need to convince them. Both Johan and Tim have advanced degrees in scientific fields, so they know way more than I do with my English literature degrees. They are here because they want to help us maintain this meadow as a home for birds. The plan they will use in the application will involve mowing half the fields multiple times a season while treating the thistle and parsnip. "But leave some of the knapweed," Tim declares. "The insects like it and it's pretty." I'm no longer wowed by pretty. I want the knapweed gone too, before the meadow turns purple, but don't say anything. I can live with some knapweed. During this treatment, the birds will have to move into the other half of the meadow and make do with more crowded quarters for a few seasons. I'm not convinced about the intensive mowing, but figure it's best to say nothing for now. Maybe for a year, so the invasives can be easily spotted and dealt with.

Before they leave, they quickly solve a puzzle that has kept us wondering for years. Why are half the fields badly invaded while the upper halves, the ones closer to the road, less so, even though it stands to reason that they would be more invaded given the easy path from neighboring fields into ours?

"Which way does the wind blow?" asks Tim.

Of course. Almost always from the southwest, bringing rafts of seeds and leaving them scattered over the lower fields. By the time the wind reaches the upper fields, it has been slowed by the hilltop, but no matter: it has already dropped most of its cargo before reaching the top.

Tim leaves with some disease-ridden apples, and Johan with one of the dozen massive Cinderella pumpkins that grew unbidden, hogging the vegetable garden. So much for weeding success, even in a tightly controlled garden.

I worry about this radical solution. The meadow, like all ecosystems, is held together by the dynamic interactions between species. When we start undoing these strands, things start to unravel, and we can't predict or control the ways. Nature is self-determining, self-willed, wild. The invasive non-native weeds, once launched into this land, are now part of the ecosystem, which has a will and momentum of its own. It's one thing to pull or spray individual plants, to in effect weed the meadow; it's another to turn it into a lawn.

But there seems to be little choice. And hope is what sustains gardeners, whether it's a couple of tomato plants or acres of meadow.

# 16 THE SHAKESPEARE GARDEN

Tucked away in the northern reaches of New York City's Central Park is a hidden garden. That is, if anything can be hidden in a park visited by forty-three million people a year. The four-acre Shakespeare Garden, designed to evoke the Bard's native English countryside, features many of the plants mentioned in his works. It was one of my favorite haunts when I worked in Midtown Manhattan, an almost quiet retreat where I could unwind for a bit amid seasonal color.

Since it's designed to be an English garden, the majority of the plants are by definition not native to North America. The garden is an entirely man-made creation, and like all professionally designed and meticulously tended gardens, it's beautiful and ever changing. Spring is especially alluring with swaths of tulips, daffodils, hellebores, and fritillaries.

But it's more than that. It's a haven not only to me but to countless insects and birds. Resting on a rustic bench after my thirty-block walk, half-hidden under a spreading shrub, I would be entertained by a steady stream of butterflies, birds, and unknown insects, all of whom ignored me as they went about their lives. None seemed to care that the flowers they visited or the seeds they ate were non-native. They seemed as happy as I was in this artificial garden.

All of Central Park is itself a man-made creation. Once, the nearly nine hundred acres were home to small farms, industrial enterprises, and dwellings scattered between wetland and rocky hills. All the sweeping lawns, picturesque woodlands, meandering streams, and broad lakes are man-made, and many or most of its plants hail from other continents. It was the genius of its designers, Frederick Law Olmsted and Calvert B. Vaux, that it appears as a natural environment turned into a park rather than the other way around.

And yet the park provides significant ecological benefits. Its more than eighteen thousand trees cool and clean the air, and the vast greenness in the center of the city provides habitat for wildlife, including as a stopover on the Atlantic Flyway for over two hundred species of birds.

The Shakespeare Garden fits perfectly into the park at large and contributes an outsize share to its value.

As does William Shakespeare to the world at large. The bestselling author in the history of the world, Shakespeare is revered and enjoyed by multiple millions around the globe. Does his popularity detract from the various cultures where his plays are performed? Does it discourage homegrown poets, playwrights, and novelists from writing their own great works? Does any culture think less of its native writers because they also admire Shakespeare? Or are both the native writers and the native culture enriched by Shakespeare's genius?

Like the Asian tulips and daffodils that embellish the Shakespeare Garden, or the Japanese cherry blossoms that draw millions of visitors to Washington, DC, every spring, non-native plants—and poets—enrich our culture and our individual lives.

# 17

# IN WHICH WE REACH AN IMPASSE

Summers, we have lots of company. Family and old friends from the New York City area and from across the country come, from Colorado and Los Angeles and as far as Oregon. Everyone wants to come in July and August. We try to convince them that we do not live in an Arctic climate, that it's almost as warm in June and September, but it doesn't work. Then we say only children and teachers can come in July and August, but there are always extenuating circumstances.

Everyone comes just when we need to be out in the meadow daily, dealing with the worst of the weeds. Which at one time seemed like a lucky coincidence, since guests could contribute to the effort. I wouldn't expect them to spend hours in the sun, dressed in long sleeves, long pants, and socks. I would ask for an hour, after breakfast maybe, when it's not so hot, or before lunch, or simply leave it up to them. I wouldn't want to get in the way of their relaxation, sightseeing, swimming, biking, or simply sitting and enjoying the scenery they all so appreciate.

But guests rise late; they are, after all, on vacation. And they drink their coffee at a leisurely pace, sitting on the patio, staring at the Adirondacks, which are bathed in late morning sun. Then they catch up on the day's news, and eventually begin the conversation about how best to spend yet another perfect day in Vermont.

Meanwhile, Ted and I had been out weeding since early morning. We are not missed. The guests can see us a hundred feet below them. But they don't see us. Their eyes are gazing into the great blue distances.

Eventually we walk up and greet them. They look surprised. We kick off shoes, grab a drink, and sit down next to them. They confirm they slept excellently. They feel energetic, just great, really. Rearing to go. What do we think they should do today?

What do we think? We think they should join us in our labor. I invite them to join us, just for an hour maybe? Then we can go to the lake, bring the kayaks and the float. I entice further with a picnic lunch with fresh raspberries; there are many ripening and ready to be picked.

Sure, they agree. Great idea. And they volunteer to pick the raspberries. Later.

We return to the poison parsnip. There are enough of them to keep me fully engaged, a whole hillside of large mustard-yellow heads bobbing in the breeze, mocking me. But I am distracted by the Canada thistle, which is well into its adolescent growth spurt, its hormones going berserk as it reaches up with its spindly torso, the flower still a tight cluster pinched at the top, its roots pulsating with energy, elbowing, ramming into great distances. And by the knapweed, which began its invasion into our meadow with a modest patch, which I didn't notice until it bloomed in late summer with rather pretty purple flowers. Now the patches have multiplied vastly, and the flowers appear glaring. Knapweed cannot be pulled like parsnip, or even like thistle, which is several orders of difficulty beyond the much larger parsnip. I decide to ignore both for now. Ted is waving to me, then moving his arms briskly to signal that he's done. When I don't respond, hoping he'll do a little more, seeing how I, the weaker sex, am not yet giving up, he yells.

"I'm done!

"Done!" he repeats, waving his arms scissorlike in case I missed it.

And that's how our weeding relationship functions. He sets strict boundaries on the circumstances and the limits of his participation in the weed wars, while trying to restrain me from "going overboard" and becoming "obsessive." He looks amused as I slide down in the car seat, trying to avoid seeing the parsnips lined up a dozen deep along every road. Eyes scrunched tightly, I try not to moan. "Tell me when it's over," I want to say, as I do when violence is about to take place in a movie we're watching, but it feels too dramatic. On a trip to visit our daughter in Portland, Oregon, we take long walks, admiring the stunning gardens spilling out of every front yard, gardens filled with tree-sized rhododendron, roses, lavender, iris, and many plants I don't know well because they don't grow in New England. And with weeds, which also reach unnatural heights in the daily rains. Ted has to physically restrain me from yanking out a weed or two or more as we pass by the yards. I am to walk on the side away from the houses and the gardens.

Back home, I search for more powerful (read: younger) and more committed assistance with our weeds. I, too, am worn out with hours of hard labor in summer heat and humidity. I spread the word among people I know and put calls for paid help in the local Listserv, calls that basically say "name your price." And it works. A young man calls to say he and his friend are willing to give it a try. Which they do, the very next day, a weekday, which might mean that they are not fully employed. They arrive, looking clean and energetic, friendly and cheerful.

They walk into the tall grass with us so we can show them what needs to happen. It's soon clear that even though they're native Vermonters, they know nothing about plants. I try to explain the logic behind the work, pointing out the danger these parsnips pose to our thriving meadow and its avian residents. How otherwise can I whip up any enthusiasm? They nod agreeably but look bored. They start to work. I bring ice water and raspberries we picked that morning. At noon, I bring a selection of sandwiches and more water. Also my outrageous flourless chocolate cookies. By two o'clock they're quitting. They promise to come back before the end of week, they'll let us know. They don't call us, so we call them. They don't return our calls.

This scenario is repeated just one more time, because we only get one other response.

When we lived in the New York metropolitan area, Spanish-speaking immigrants waited in specific sites such as the commuter parking lot, where people came to hire them for a day's work. We occasionally brought one or two of these strong young men to help with maintenance jobs, and found them to be hardworking and honest. But they were not in Vermont, or at least not in our part of Vermont, which is relatively rural with few housing options. But they were living just a few miles west in New York's small upstate towns. We could drive there, take a walk, and with my rudimentary Spanish, chat them up and see if they might be interested in helping us. It seemed like a practical arrangement. We get help, they get money. What could possibly be wrong with it?

A lot, apparently.

"Really, Mom!" my daughter raises her voice, a rare occurrence and a sign of true emotion. But I don't understand.

"You're going to hire people they call 'illegal aliens' to tear out alien plants! Can't you see the problem here?"

"Well . . ." I try. "You're focusing on symbolism that has nothing to do with the issue at hand, which is really very simple. We need help!"

I'm not successful at convincing her.

My escape is a corner of our property where a small forest grows taller and wider each year. Except for that, the changes here are not in-your-face, as they are in the meadow. Young pines, maples, and poplars spring up around the perimeter, and they grow rapidly, expanding the forest into the surrounding meadow. We allow this; there is plenty of meadow and little forest. Beyond the perimeter, where the apple trees still live, the trees in the little forest are tall, shutting out the light, so there are few saplings. The forest is a world unto itself, closed to everything outside it—including the invasives moving into the meadow. The trees move outward into the meadow, but the meadow doesn't move in.

"The woods are lovely, dark and deep" explains why it stays weed free. Weeds are a sun-loving lot. There is little sun in a forest for poison parsnip or Canada thistle or knapweed. Not even for the poplars and boxelders that are beginning to expand their range, in the tall grass, bent on becoming a young forest. The forest is a staid old-boys clubhouse, filled with deep leather chairs and floor-to-ceiling dark curtains. Only members and children of members allowed. No flowers, shrubs, or trees barging in, and certainly no non-natives, pushy immigrants that would forever alter the whole dank atmosphere.

No immigrant plants in virgin prairie either. The roots of prairie grass are so close no upstarts can get in. Another network of good old boys.

The forest is a living example of what I've been reading about and what should be obvious: to be invaded, a community needs to be invasible. Once, when this meadow was a forest, it was not invasible. When it was cut, it became wildly attractive to whatever weeds held sway back in the 1800s, when it was first turned into pasture. The sheep that roamed the new pasture kept everything in check. Upstart trees were promptly chewed down, and even the grass was kept at lawn height. The cows that followed the sheep continued to munch, chew, and grind. The apple trees in the orchard it eventually became cast enough shade to keep many weeds out even as the cows continued to live and graze in the orchard. Shade and repeated destruction by the animals gave invasive weeds no chance to flourish. But once we had the orchard cut down and asked the farmer to remove his cows so we could move around freely, the new meadow became a free-for-all. We put out the invitation, and every plant with an eye for opportunity accepted. They came from everywhere, many likely from seeds buried in the earth for decades, dormant, biding their time. The fact that we want to maintain it in the state it was in right after it became a meadow is our choice.

At the same time, the insects, birds, and other indigenous wildlife need their food, which is often present only on the native plants that populate the meadow. The insects especially need our meadow. The world's vital insect kingdom is being rapidly decimated, a process so dramatic it's called the insect apocalypse. Climate change, insecticides, herbicides, changes in agriculture and land use, and even light pollution are causing the loss of 1 to 2 percent of earth's insects each year, according to a report by the National Academies of Science signed by fifty-six scientists from around the globe titled "Insect Decline in the Anthropocene: Death by a Thousand Cuts" and published on January 12, 2020.

Monarch butterflies are among the insects that best illustrate the decline. Every monarch butterfly is hatched on the leaf of a milkweed plant, a native flower in short supply. Once ubiquitous in fields, empty lots, along roadsides, and at the edges of farms, milkweed has been decimated by development and herbicides. Monarch numbers have followed its decline, dropping from a billion twenty years ago to only ninety-three million today. Our meadow is a riot of milkweed. It's just one meadow though. The first fall we owned this property, less than two decades ago, I was out on a bike ride. Clouds of monarchs floated toward me, and I stopped to let them pass. Soon I was biking through another, bigger cloud, and I got off the bike and was afraid to get back on, afraid to move, afraid of hitting the frail orange apparitions, afraid a touch of metal or skin would injure the gossamer wings. These days, the clouds have been reduced to straggling individuals leaving on their inconceivably long migration to their Mexican wintering grounds. If the monarchs make it back to our meadow next year, they will have plenty of milkweed on which to grow a new generation, because the milkweeds keep expanding their numbers, apparently loving the conditions in our meadow. But milkweeds need a meadow to grow.

Other, lesser-known butterflies are also declining, with thirty-two species on the federal Endangered Species Act list, and many more imperiled grass-feeding butterflies that are not yet on the list. Habitat loss is the leading cause. More than 99 percent of grasslands have been lost in some areas, which makes species-diverse, native-flower-rich grasslands like ours a precious asset.

Many non-native flowers don't offer the same lifeline to insects and birds. Take the multiflora rose, native to Asia, which may just be getting a foothold in the meadow. Even though its berries look delicious to our birds, they lack nutrition, thus doing more harm than good.

"It's like the birds getting a candy bar versus getting something more substantial, something with more protein in it, some more fat in it. And those empty calories hurt birds' ability to migrate or survive the winter," explains Vasiliy Lakoba of Virginia Tech. Another non-native plant, our problematic spotted knapweed, he points out, actually hurts insects. Its small leaves and wild branching provide excellent scaffolding for spiders, and those spiders catch a lot of insects that would be eating the knapweed and suppressing its population. A preemptive strike by the knapweed.

In the photo that accompanies Lakoba's article, all the team members are holding pretty bouquets of non-native invasive weeds.

Pretty simply doesn't cut it. Land needs to offer beauty and sustenance. Our meadow does that. It earns our devotion and our labor. Yes, labor. I rail at the laws of nature, of natural succession, which refuse to conform to our dreams. Then I find myself moving into my daughter's camp. The weeds are ours, and ours to deal with. No immigrants to kill immigrant weeds.

# 18

# WEEDING

Writing a book is a lot like gardening.

You don't begin a garden with planting. Before burying a seed or digging a hole for a plant, there's the research: the slope of the site, the angle of the sun, the makeup of the soil. Careful planning follows, of drawing shapes on paper and earth, of stringing lines, of mounding soil and removing rocks. Finally, you get to choose among the pages of tomatoes and lettuce in the seed catalogs, or the promise of baby shrubs and trees in the nursery.

You don't begin a book with writing. Before putting word on screen, you spend months or years learning about your subject, an endeavor called research. You read about your subject almost exclusively, allowing yourself only one long news article a day and a few pages of a novel at night.

Finally, you begin to write. Maybe you have an outline, the equivalent of a garden design. You know that neither the writing nor the planting will hew to the plan, that both will ignore the logical flow of information and the meticulously drawn shapes. But it's the right and proper way to go about a huge project, and you want the book and the garden to be right and proper.

It's not your fault. Chance, serendipity, and the randomness of life all conspire to thwart logic and plan, like the minuscule lettuce and carrot seeds you plant, kneeling in the chill earth, trying so hard to spread them out evenly, with stiff fingers, with the pasta strainer, with a special seed dropper. But when the carrots and lettuce show their first tender leaves, they are clumped in places and absent from others. There's either too much or too little. The carefully laid rows are a twisted rope. You need to reseed some areas but you've used up the packet. You start over.

You have the same problems with the book. There's too much or too little information, or it remains unclear or there is not enough freshness or beauty. Some parts are dense; others don't hold together at all.

Then you know it's time to weed.

You get down to the still-chill earth. You are determined to pull out enough seedlings to give the remaining ones the room you know they need. It feels like murder. You leave in more than you should, thinking you will pull them when they've grown a bit and can go in a fresh salad. You transplant some of the seedlings into bare areas. These will die, and you know it.

The book, too, needs weeding. The book, too, you weed on your hands and knees. You lay out all the pages on the floor, since there's no table large enough to hold them. For days you scramble on all fours like a toddler. You weed out pages, whole sections. You dig out, you discard, you move some. You've spent hours writing a sentence or two, days writing sections, and you love them, you are in love with your words. But they'll die if you move them where they don't belong. So you weed them out. It feels like murder. Then you have to fill in the gaping emptinesses that are left. That takes a long time. You insist the papers covering the floor must stay where they are. No one can visit. You are weeding a book.

You spend more days on the floor. By now you're scuttling sideways crablike, your knees having been rubbed raw. Except you don't have multiple legs, so your right hip is taking the brunt. Every night you take a hot bath. Then you lie on a heating pad, which, being exhausted from all the scuttling and crawling, you forget to turn off until you wake to singed skin and extreme perspiration. Then you take a shower. You're very clean at this stage of the book.

One day, the carrots, the lettuce, and the book are close to where they should be. Never the perfection you envisioned. But edible. Readable. Maybe even delicious and quite good.

Dear Reader:

Just sayin' . . .

# HOW TO BECOME NATIVE

*For on no other ground*
*Can I sow my seed,*
*Without tearing up*
*Some stinking weed.*
—WILLIAM BLAKE,
*Poems from the Rossetti Manuscript*

How does one become American?

This was the question that occupied my mind through my teenage years. At thirteen, when we arrived in New York Harbor on a frigid February day, I was not preoccupied with my appearance. My family thought I was beautiful, but I logically dismissed that. I thought I was moderately pretty with no glaring physical faults beyond the ordinary imperfect nose and teenage skin.

But my first day in school in the South Bronx, which was where we were taken right off the boat, taught me otherwise. I was all wrong. Wrong color, since I was the only white face among the Black and Brown faces. Wrong, terribly wrong clothes. Wrong hairdo. Even my personal hygiene was suspect, as I learned in gym class, since I was not yet shaving my legs or underarms. And, of course, there was the matter of language. Less than two years of English class in Israel hardly prepared me for tackling "Romeo and Juliet," or, more importantly, for making conversation or friends.

It didn't take very long to learn how to *look* like an acceptable American teenager. Feeling like one, however, took longer than my adolescence lasted. When tapped to join a popular clique in high school, I demurred. I didn't fit; I had not mastered the codes; I lacked cultural reference points; slang often eluded me; my conversation was stilted, odd, since I was learning it from books. I was not yet American, and I didn't know that it would take years longer to become one.

I remembered my long road to becoming American when I read about Ford's English School. It turns out, automobiles were not the only product produced in the assembly lines in Ford's factories. Newly minted "Americans" were another product.

The Henry Ford English School was designed to turn out Americans in the same way it turned out cars. Founded in 1914, immigrant workers were taught English but also the Yankee values of thrift, cleanliness, community, and punctuality. (The latter very much persists in Vermont. Why, otherwise, would anyone show up for dinner at precisely the set time? It's positively rude!) Once these values were successfully mastered, the graduates would qualify for the "five-dollar day" that was considered a living wage.

At the graduation ceremony, students dressed in the national costume of their home countries paraded down the gangway of a mock ship and into a huge cauldron labeled the "melting pot," which the teachers stirred with enormous spoons. Afterward the new Americans marched out in suits and ties and waving American flags. They had become American.

The melting pot may not have been instant, but the waves of immigrants who arrived between 1830 and 1924 were in fact absorbed into the dominant culture. Whatever influence they had on the national culture was regional, limited to just a few locations, mainly the gateway cities of New York, Philadelphia, Boston, Chicago, and San Francisco. Even as aspects of different cultures remained in ethnic foods, expressions, and religions, these remained mostly within the confines of the original immigration centers and did not profoundly influence the dominant Anglo-Protestant culture. The melting pot was, for a while at least, highly efficient.

It seems that it takes significantly longer for an immigrant plant to become American than it took Ford's workers. There is no melting pot cauldron they enter to exit as full-fledged Americans. It's not at all clear when foreign plants achieve native status.

In the United States, "native" often means plants that were here before 1492. The arrival of Europeans went hand in hand with the arrival of European flora. And just as the pre-Columbian population had no weapon against the diseases Europeans brought, so the native flora was crushed by the success of the foreign flora. Or so the argument goes. In fact, pre-Columbian Americans domesticated plants and engaged in long-distance trade, moving them around the continent. They also practiced large-scale gardening by regular burning, sowing, pruning, and harvesting.

The newly arrived plants that came with the early settlers seem to have been accepted as part of the landscape rather quickly, at least by average folk who liked the cheerful dandelions, the medicinally useful plantains, and the impressive and delicious parsnip. But as plants from around the world arrived at an increasing pace, they began to be viewed less warmly. American attitudes toward immigrant plants and immigrant people took a turn around the same time.

The exception was and remains grass. A third of residential water use goes to our lawns and gardens, plus an unknown quantity of human labor and an unknown quantity of carbon emitted into the atmosphere to keep lawns looking like the uninterrupted green carpets we admire. And we seem not to mind lawns' invasive tendencies, easily forgiving their encroachment on our carefully constructed flower and vegetable gardens.

"The lawn is arguably the most foolish, destructive, annoying entity on earth," insists *Wall Street Journal* columnist Joe Queenan. "Like the icebox or the harpsichord, lawns are a useless vestige of a bygone era."

Grass and lawns, I was thinking, show that our concept of non-native invasives is driven by ideas rooted more in culture than in science.

This new turn in my thinking was making me feel beneficent toward our particular weeds. Also, it was November, when the outdoors is far less beckoning than in July. In November, the meadow is in a state of stasis. The grass has barely begun to regrow after being brushhogged the previous month, and the weeds, while visible in the short grass, are small and non-threatening. Looking at a thistle in its infant state I can easily visualize it in its powerful prime. But for now I try not to. I need a rest as much as the thistle.

Instead of searching for ways to eradicate, I read about perfection. Not the perfection of gardens, a Japanese one, for example, which I've admired with an unexplainable longing ever since I became aware of gardens as art. Instead I read about the supposed perfection of the world's landscapes in some moment in the very distant past. A time after the breakup of the supercontinent Pangaea, when the structure of our planet, with its continents separated by ocean, would have kept most plants in their original homes. When everything was growing exactly where it was meant to, fully belonging in its original home. In this moment, everything was native and also exotic, because each place was unique and different from every other place.

When was this perfect frozen moment? It must have been before humans arrived, a blink of an eye ago in earth's history. But most likely there was never such a moment, not even before humans began to harness nature to their own ends.

That's because the earth is too dynamic to permit any natural environment to become permanent. Earthquakes, floods, volcanic eruptions, tornadoes, hurricanes, tsunamis, fires, and other geologic processes, as well as repeated ice ages, ensure that whole ecosystems are regularly transformed.

Species are born, spread, and die. They may expand in their original birthplace or spread into a range that doesn't include their original home, as happens on newly formed islands. Their range may be continuous or broken up into small or giant patches. They may live a million years or less or many millions. Eventually, though, they die.

Once humans arrived and began putting their stamp on the natural world, growing some plants, attempting to eradicate others, and finally spreading them around the globe, all bets were off. "Nature" is not natural, being managed by humans as it is. Natural history and human history are one and the same.

This renders our notion of the "rightness" or the "belonging" of certain species in specific geographic locations irrelevant. It means that the very concept of "native" is flawed. It means that whatever is growing is growing in the right spot. It means that the plants we consider alien today are the natives of tomorrow. Much like the children of newly arrived Americans rapidly become . . . American. It means that being native—for plants and for people—is a matter of chance, of landing in one place instead of another. It means that we belong exactly where we are.

Ted and I landed here because I had a deep and irrational desire to own a large piece of land. Not just any land, but land with distant views, with water for growing food and beauty, with sugar maple trees for tapping for syrup, with unimpeded sun and privacy. But also with a town, a community to belong to, and, last but not least, within our means. A long list for sure, but there had to be thousands of such places for sale in the Northeast. The fact that we landed on this particular hill is a result of pure chance and some persistence on our part. Once here, we made this place our home, where we belong as much as we would anywhere else or as much as anyone else would belong here.

Like the plants that are continually moving in and changing our mutable landscape, we, too, are altering it to suit our vision.

What, I wondered, would our meadow look like if we killed everything now growing on it, then sat back and did nothing, just allowed nature to take its course? It would not look as it did a century ago when it was pasture for domestic animals. Nor as it did after we had the apple trees cut. There would be grass, sure, and the old standbys. Dandelions would arrive first, followed by milkweed, buttercup, golden Alexander, vetch, clover, daisies, black-eyed Susan, dwarf cinquefoil, and pussytoes. But along with these original inhabitants would come the whole host of gate-crashers, from other places and from the seeds that had been lying patiently in the soil waiting for their chance at life, seeds from the meadow, from the recent orchard, from the old pasture and the older forest. Some would live in peace; others would be rampant in their ambition to conquer every inch of ground by hooked seed and crooked root. Would they, too, be in the right place? Would they also belong?

# 20
## REALLY?

Don't get me wrong. I love New York City's Highline, the nearly two-mile-long elevated linear park, greenway, and rail trail created on a former railroad spur. It's a priceless addition to the city, brilliantly landscaped by the master of "natural landscaping" Piet Oudolf. In a nod to the wild weeds that sprung up during the twenty-five years that the land was abandoned, Oudolf had it planted with grasses, wildflowers, native shrubs, and small trees. It's a wildflower meadow, prairie, and woodland. It's how our meadow would look—if we had a contingent of gardeners to work it daily.

I love it. I am also unreasonably envious. Unreasonably because, as garden writer Emma Marris explains, "Ironically for a park that sprang from an appreciation of the feral and untended, it now has the highest maintenance costs of any park in the city." Well, of course! How could it look anything but magnificent?

It's not just the maintenance though. While the design is said to have been inspired by wildness, the Highline started out as a blank slate after everything was scraped away. No weed seeds buried in soil survived. Only then was everything planted. The fact that it looks like nature's work is a tribute to Oudolf's genius, a style of gardening called "enhanced nature."

It seems everyone wants a native meadow these days. It's a style of gardening that fits wonderfully into the popular natural landscaping style. I have read a number of books and watched webinars and lectures on the wonders of meadows: the food and shelter they provide pollinators; their "naturalness," because they put back what nature intended (really?); that meadows do away with the need for weekly mowing (true); that they are low-maintenance (no way!). At the end of each session, I ask the same question: What about the (unmentioned) weeds?

The answers range from "If you do it right from the beginning . . ." and "It hasn't been a problem" to "You have to get them early."

"Why have wildflower meadows not become a staple of the American landscape?" asks Larry Weaner, a recognized meadow expert. "Designed meadows have been available for years and have received great amounts of publicity. Claims that they can provide a carpet of beautiful flowers, with little or no maintenance, would seem to make them an ideal solution. They have not proliferated because all too often they have failed."

And, he might have added, because they are far, very far, from low-maintenance.

# 21 THE FIRST AND PRESENT BEAUTY

*The beauty of the earth is the first beauty. Millions of years before us, the earth lived in wild elegance.*
—JOHN O'DONOHUE,
*Beauty: The Invisible Embrace*

We have a friend who has lived in Manhattan her entire adult life. She admires everything about the city: its architecture and parks, its elegant neighborhoods and its gritty sections, its multitudes of humans. She even finds New York City's subway system attractive and safe, and rides it alone at any time of day or night.

She came to visit us one summer soon after we moved to Vermont. She stayed mostly inside, unless we planned an outing somewhere. Then she walked quickly from house to car. She did not want to walk around outside our house and see the beauty we saw. On the second day she finally worked up her courage and went to sit in one of the Adirondack chairs, but spent the time reading her book, rarely raising her eyes from the page.

We were puzzled but not hurt. Our friend explained that she didn't feel comfortable in such a big open space. What was she afraid of, we inquired as empathetically as we could. Animals. Big animals, small animals, and strange insects frightened her. Even inside the house, with the doors left unlocked day and night, she felt threatened.

We didn't ask if she found our meadow and woods, the distant views of the Adirondack High Peaks, or the close views of the multitudes of wildflowers then blooming beautiful. We knew she did not. Everything was so daunting compared to the subway at midnight. And absent people, architectural marvels, and noise, possibly boring. Nothing to look at.

I was remembering this weekend as I wandered through the meadow hunting for early blackberries. Wild blackberries grow pretty white flowers, which then turn into glistening dark fruit, which, even better, are luscious, delicious, and good for you. In the fall, the shrubs turn a deep burgundy. Bears like them too. I know this because I can see their paths through the thickets, which I'm not above taking advantage of myself. So do skunks, red foxes, and raccoons. Woodpeckers, robins, cardinals, kingbirds, tanagers, sparrows, and many more birds feast on blackberries in the fall; even in winter, after the fruit have fallen to the ground, birds eat the seeds that remain when the fruit decomposes.

But. Blackberries are invasive, aggressive, nasty shrubs, and also non-native. Left alone, they would rapidly colonize the meadow, becoming so overgrown and dense that no bear or human could enjoy their fruit, whose seeds would be used strictly for expansion purposes.

Objectively speaking, blackberry shrubs are no less attractive than the cultivated raspberries I planted and that I water, weed, and thin out as needed. But, subjectively, I find them distressingly unattractive.

Which raises the question: What kind of nature is beautiful?

On a trip to Portugal, we joined a group of tourists to visit the country's famous cork forests. The southern Mediterranean soil and climate are perfect for cork oak, and 80 percent of the world's cork is grown in Portugal. Used mostly as stoppers for wine bottles, cork is also used in bulletin boards, wall and floor tiles, and other lesser-known products. I am the proud owner of a cork bag. Cork is the country's national tree, protected by stiff laws.

I had seen pictures of cork forests. Thousands of trees, their limbs spreading elegantly, their branches held in ballet's fifth position, their furrowed bark sculpted by time and weather. I was looking forward to wandering among the trees, learning about them, sitting under an especially old and large one to enjoy our picnic lunch. It was to be an afternoon spent in a beautiful forest of the kind I'd probably never see again.

So I was shocked to find myself more than disappointed. Seriously repelled. Cork products are made from the bark of the trees, bark that is peeled off the trunk. When trees are twenty-five years old, a cut is made about halfway up the trunk, and the thick bark or cork layer is peeled off, leaving the raw reddish-brown wood exposed. This is carefully timed, done every nine years, and the peeled trees are inscribed with the date of the last peel. The trees continue to live for as long as two hundred years, unharmed.

But I was struck by what looked to me like mutilation, not at all like harvesting apples from trees. While others in our group listened to the biologist describe the process, I was focused on the missing bark. "It's like peeling our skin!" I whispered to Ted. But the Portuguese are proud of their unique forests, and some of the rich choose to build their homes among them, evidently not bothered by the peeled trees, finding them beautiful.

Surely beauty is in the eye of the beholder, whether looking at a tree, a person, or a car. But the contrasts are puzzling.

My mother grew roses and azaleas in the diminutive "garden" outside our attached brick house. She liked the roses too much to ever trim them, so they grew and grew, hung on nails attached to the brick, splayed over the air conditioner, reaching over the fence. Blooms were few, so the mess could be ignored. But the azaleas could not. They were a lurid fuchsia, and when in bloom, they pulsed menacingly. To my mother, the more electric and the bigger the shrubs grew, the better. But my father, being a tailor, liked to trim things with the large shears he had carried across three continents. Every spring, after wielding the shears over the "lawn" until the few dozen blades were cut to the height of grass in a golf course, he would turn to the azaleas. This would be just when they were at their most glaring intensity. He would begin trimming the offending shrubs, circling them, cutting branches, then cutting the ones that stuck out, circling one last time before moving to the next shrub. He never stepped back to view his handiwork, not until all three shrubs were in a state he considered appropriately neat. When my mother returned from grocery shopping, the devastation that greeted her would launch the annual azalea war, with each insisting on the rightness of his or her aesthetic vision.

I was trying to imagine our meadow as it would look after a decade of no attention. What if we embraced the dynamism of change and let the winners go on winning? A field of invasive weeds, followed by a brushland of invasive shrubs, and finally a young forest of boxelder, poplar, and red maple, maybe a few of the iconic New England ancients: sugar maple, birch, beech, red oak, white pine. No ash, because the emerald ash borer, which arrived here a couple of years ago, will have finished off the ash trees well before then.

It would be far from a native landscape, being at best a combination of a few original settlers and new arrivals, some legitimately invited, others crashing the gates. But from what I was learning in my reading, it would be a thriving ecosystem. Because, contrary to expectation, when it comes to nature, the more the merrier.

When the field of invasion biology was born in the 1950s, the fear was that the growing armies of non-native invasives would proliferate and soon replace the native plants. This was not a far-fetched idea given that new arrivals have distinct and powerful advantages. They have no natural enemies. No devastating insects have evolved to destroy them in their new environment. No local pathogens are ready to decimate them either. And landing in a novel environment, the new plants quickly change their internal clocks, maturing earlier than the native population, spreading their seeds and roots while the natives are just waking from their winter dormancy.

But the "10 percent rule" puts that fear to rest. It says that of all non-native species that are released into new ecosystems, only about 10 percent survive, and of these survivors, about 10 percent (or just 1 percent of the original number of species released) become invasive. And unlike clear-cutting a forest or poisoning a river, non-native invasions don't make ecosystems disappear. In fact, in many cases, ecosystems stand to benefit. As we continue to destroy habitats, the newcomers are filling in the empty spots we create. And contrary to expectations, they are doing so without major impact on the plants already there.

"Most invasive species don't appear to be having that much of an impact on local biodiversity," writes Garry Hamilton in *Super Species*. New evidence shows that heavily invaded environments worldwide are in fact showing a surprising increase in diversity. So "instead of destroying the biosphere, invasive species may be creating a new one from the rubble of our destruction."

Puerto Rico illustrates this concept on the ground. The island has a long history of environmental abuse. What was once a dense tropical rain forest has been denuded over the centuries since Columbus landed there. Then, in the middle of the twentieth century, social shifts caused the farms and plantations to be abandoned, leaving about half the island open to whatever nature wrought. By then, even the earth was not what it had once been, consisting of drained wetlands, clogged rivers, and compacted soil. The empty land lay scorched under the tropical sun.

Non-native species that had been brought to the island over time suddenly found their place in the sun. These were the wildly proliferating tulip and guava trees, rose apple, and white iris, which spreads up to seventeen acres a year. They were mostly from the stock of introduced species. Was this better than drained, compacted, raw earth?

Certainly, a green ecosystem is preferable to desiccated, bare earth. But it was better than that.

It turned out the non-natives were paving the way for the natives' return. They broke up and enriched the dry compacted soil. They provided a home for birds and insects, which spread the seeds of both native and non-native plants, filling up the empty spaces, creating a new forest. Although these forests contain many non-native species, few are dominated by them. Furthermore, these forests are wealthier in species, creating greater diversity. Some 750 different tree species are now growing in Puerto Rico, compared to the 547 estimated to be present during pre-Columbian times, a 20 percent increase. The newcomers have ended up producing new forests that are different from the old ones, but that are functioning biodiverse natural ecosystems. There is even a new word—ecosynthesis—for these mixtures of native and foreign species.

Similar processes have been observed in other places. Sixty years ago, there was a large patch of abandoned agricultural land in Ohio. The farmers had moved on, leaving the plowed land empty, open to whatever wanted to move in. At first, the land was dominated by European and Asian natives that tended toward colonizing behavior. Japanese honeysuckle, bindweed, wild carrot, and multiflora rose were abundant. But as succession proceeded, their numbers kept decreasing. Now a forest covers the land. As the trees continue to grow, they are shading out the non-native plants, while animals and pathogens have finally caught up with them as well. The moral? The best way to get rid of invasives—at least in forests—is to ignore them. If you can wait long enough.

Newly formed islands dramatically demonstrate nature's resilience and non-natives' positive impact. These islands are rapidly colonized by plants and animals that travel from near and far, on birds and wind and spider silk, rapidly producing rich ecosystems. The exclusion zone around the stricken Chernobyl nuclear reactor in Ukraine is a sort of island and a lesson in nature's regenerative powers. The area is still radioactive, and no humans are allowed to live in it. But nature has positively reveled in the absence of humans. Far from being a postapocalyptic desert, it's a thriving ecosystem of both original and new species. The absence of people has allowed not only plants but also wildlife to become more abundant. The animals even take advantage of human dwellings, using them extensively as hiding places and homes to raise their young, as well as to feed themselves from the overgrown human gardens. They may die earlier, but wild animals rarely die of old age anyway.

Nor is there evidence that new species reduce the number of native ones. Only three of New Zealand's native plant species have been lost, while two thousand non-native plants have made their home among them. In California, out of approximately six thousand species, more than one thousand are naturalized citizens. Yet fewer than ten natives are known to have become extinct. The game of plants is unlike that of musical chairs, in which too many players compete for too few chairs. Even established ecosystems that appear quite full are able to absorb non-natives.

I'm no math whiz, but this I understand: if you add many new species and subtract none or only a few, the overall species count goes up.

"Ecosystems are not superorganisms or grand associations of species drawn inevitably to a particular 'climax,'" concludes environmental writer Fred Pearce. "They can assemble anywhere, however species like, and in whatever form works. They have no preordained template. No guest list."

I read about Andrew MacDougall, a biologist at the University of Guelph in Ontario and his studies of invasive weeds in two degraded areas that he tried to restore. The first and more interesting one was a protected property on Vancouver Island. Despite being protected, the native vegetation was failing while invasive grasses were flourishing. After the grasses were removed, MacDougall expected the native plants to reclaim their turf. But there was little change. The native plants continued to decline while woody plants began to encroach, changing the character of what was once an open savanna-like area.

He concluded that the invasives were merely moving in where the natives were already declining. And rather than hastening their decline, these new arrivals were helping keep the ecosystem closer to the original open grassland habitat. They kept the seeds of trees and shrubs from getting established by preventing light from reaching the soil. It turned out the native plants declined because they rely on regular fires to clear out dead vegetation. But with development encroaching, fires must now be suppressed. Absent fires, a thick layer of litter built up, which made it difficult for the natives to thrive. The invasives, being more adaptable, didn't mind the litter. And as they flourished, they were making it possible for the native flowers, grasses, and wildlife to survive.

Given the state of our world, we need to be ready to accept and exploit the opportunities that many non-native plants, even some invasive ones, present. Which leaves Ralph Waldo Emerson's famous definition of weeds as plants whose virtues haven't yet been discovered in a much stronger position.

Despite all the positive unexpected findings, questions remain. We don't know whether these emerging ecosystems will perform the crucial functions ecosystems perform. Will they purify the air, providing the perfect mixture of oxygen and nitrogen? And purify water, too, so we can continue to drink the same ancient water that has always been on the planet? Will they limit pests and diseases? Will they cycle nutrients and recycle waste so we don't drown in the dead plants, animals, and insects that the earth produces daily? Will they create fertile soil to feed eight or more billion people?

We take these ecosystem services for granted. They just are, right? But they are vanishing. A study compiled by more than a thousand natural and social scientists in 2005 found that 60 percent of twenty-four ecosystem services are being degraded by development, agriculture, forestry, and resource extraction while also increasing poverty at one end and affluence on the other. We don't know how much worse it has become in the intervening years.

There is early evidence that in urban and suburban areas, the newcomers provide damage control, keeping life going and providing some of the ecosystem services. In rural settings, especially on neglected land, close observation is beginning to demonstrate that the non-natives often support several ecosystem services.

Many non-natives, for example, are nitrogen fixers that enrich the soil for other plants. Some, such as our hated knapweed, also increase the amount of available phosphorus in soil, a critical and hard-to-come-by nutrient for plants. And contrary to what remains a hard-held belief, many non-native species are well loved by pollinators. These include our most reviled plants: kudzu, knotweed, and thistle. In some regions of the world, including California's Central Valley, invasive non-natives are the only known source of pollen and nectar for native pollinators. With pollinators in steep decline worldwide, this is an extremely valuable service.

Because weeds have more diverse genomes, it's easier to find one with the proper genetic resistance to a given threat and create new hybrids by crossing them with existing crops. The solution to the Irish potato blight of 1845 came from a wild and weedy relative of the potato. With a wild oat found in Israel in the 1960s, scientists created a more robust, disease-resistant domesticated oat.

World population is expected to increase to almost ten billion by midcentury. More people means more food, even as warming temperatures, increased $CO_2$, drought, and desertification are expected to lower food production. Scientists are increasingly looking to the weedy relatives of our cultivated crops as a solution. These are the very weeds that have plagued farmers since humans moved out of the forest and became agriculturists. And now, thanks to a warming climate and more $CO_2$, we already know these weeds will grow ever more aggressively, outpacing our carefully cultivated crops.

Scary, yes. But instead of fighting an increasingly difficult battle, we could take advantage of those very characteristics. By crossbreeding the cultivated and the wild, we can confer on our crops tolerance to heat and drought along with faster growth, boosting harvests to feed a growing population.

Some scientists, such as Joanne Chory at the Salk Institute for Biological Studies in La Jolla, California, are actually trying to get weeds to grow even faster, bigger, and with hefty root systems that burrow deep into the earth. They expect these genetically engineered weeds to become carbon sequestration engines by sucking out a lot of carbon from the atmosphere and burying it underground. The goal is to engineer these superpowers into wheat, corn, soy, rice, cotton, and canola, which together occupy more than half of the earth's arable land. That much carbon removed from the atmosphere could, well, save the world.

"A thing is right when it tends to preserve the integrity, stability and beauty of the biotic community," is one of ecologist Aldo Leopold's well-known pronouncements. It appears that ecosynthesis can create such communities.

I was moving into the camp of those scientists, gardeners, and landscapers who welcome non-native plants. I was exercising a new sense of fairness, experimenting with a new willingness to view all as innocent until proven guilty. Unfortunately, our experience turned up too many guilty ones. It seems the 10 percent rule expands to 50 in our meadow, with most of our newcomers determined to replace the natives. No grass grows where poison parsnip thrives. Golden Alexander and New England aster vanish when Canada thistle moves in. Their vanishing drains the meadow of the native plants I see as more beautiful. Rightly or wrongly, because they are rarer or are threatened, or because their blooms are fleeting, I find purple asters and golden Alexander far more beautiful than purple thistles and golden poison parsnip.

Some scientists insist that we have no way to judge any plant's credentials. The "biophilia hypothesis" suggests that we love nature because we evolved in it, it's in our DNA, and therefore we need it for our psychological well-being. I don't find this explanation totally satisfactory. Our love for nature may be one of the greatest mysteries of life, one that even evolutionary biologists are hard-pressed to explain. What, after all, is the utility in admiring billowing grass or silver birch bark when it doesn't feed or clothe us and serves no evolutionary purpose?

It seems we love nature not just for the services it provides. We love it because it's a balm to the soul and to frayed nerves. Because it brings peace and a sense of well-being. Because it's literally health giving. And because it's beautiful.

Human movement is now rendering the continents' separateness irrelevant. We are living in a man-made Pangaea. An earth with ecosystems that will be duplicates of each other, like the Starbucks and H&Ms that feature in every one of the world's major cities will—for this human at least—be less interesting. They may be healthy and useful, but less individual and therefore less beautiful.

"The human soul is hungry for beauty; we seek it everywhere—in landscape, music, art, clothes, furniture, gardening, companionship, love, religion, and in ourselves," says poet and priest John O'Donohue.

Will we care that the natural world's beauty will be of a different kind? Will we miss the extinct? I have never seen a forest with massive chestnuts nor a street lined with arching elms. The northeastern forests appear beautiful to me, as do the London plane trees lining Manhattan's elegant streets on the Upper East Side. Our response to beauty is culturally determined and defined by the particular moment we find ourselves in. We see beauty where we are taught to see it, and we are taught to see it where it happens to be in this moment in time. Perhaps we will learn new ways of seeing, and after a time won't remember the beauty that was. Our grandchildren will likely find the brushland of non-native invasive shrubs and trees that will supplant our meadow beautiful. Or even the fields of solar panels that are rapidly replacing grazing cows in Vermont. Only we will remember the beauty these supplanted.

# 22 INTERLUDE

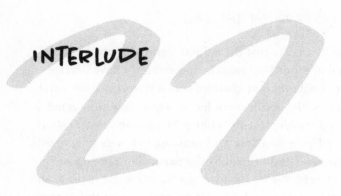

The summer of 2020 was the kind that likely inspired the saying Vermonters love to quote: "I came to Vermont for the winter but stayed for the summer."

It followed the usual endless, wet spring, really a late winter through mid-June, but when it finally arrived, it was the proverbial endless summer. Hot sun in cobalt blue sky, calm winds, and lake water whose temperature matched the air's. The sunstruck days that stretched for months were a result of a pretty serious drought, but we didn't have to worry about fires, and I didn't mind having to lug the heavy hose to every corner every other day to water the parched gardens.

The drought magically restored the meadow to its infancy.

The weeds suffered badly from the lack of rain and the daily dose of full sun. They certainly didn't die nor even dry out completely. But they grew meagerly, never reaching their full height or girth, cowering close to the ground in an effort at survival. The wildflowers suffered the same fate, so that we barely got to enjoy the evening primrose, butter-and-eggs, daisies, and black-eyed Susans, which stayed mostly hidden.

The grass, free of the wild madder stems that in other summers climb over it and bend it with their cumulative weight, rose lush in clear defiance of its suddenly lowly neighbors, its blades spearing the cobalt sky. Orchard grass, meadow fescue, timothy, and bromegrass, and many others I can't identify, grew over the vetch, clover, trefoil, and Queen Anne's lace.

We didn't miss the wildflowers. The grass alone sufficed. It took center stage, hogging all our attention.

The grass grew tall, and the blades grew thick and raspy. They towered over my head, and I had to look up to see the heavy seedpods. Walking the paths, I was enclosed in a tunnel, the walls of a fort, seeing nothing but the green. I could feel the pulse of life in the living tunnel, and feel my body responding, mirroring its vitality. Shut inside the grandeur, I could, for brief moments, become part of its life force.

From a distance, the grass rippled in staggered shiny waves, a lit sea of green raising its radiance to the sky. It gave the wind a language, spoken in soft sliding sounds and dry rubbing sounds and secret rustling sounds. All the grass sounds merged with the drunken song of the bobolinks that swayed on top of the grasses, miraculously holding on in the slaps of hot wind.

# THE SWEET SPOT

*According to Darwin's Origin of Species, it is not the most intellectual of the species that survives; it is not the strongest that survives; but the species that survives is the one that is able best to adapt and adjust to the changing environment in which it finds itself.*

—LEON C. MEGGINSON, "Lessons from Europe for American Business"

During the years we've owned this land, I've been noticing how restless the earth is, how busy transforming itself. Not just with the seasons; the sections we leave uncut are now on the cusp of brushland and the dawn of forest. We are playing no part in this drama. Natural succession is unleashing the forces that are rushing this process along.

This business of natural succession is not natural at all. It's a bloody war, with no prisoners taken. Only the victors survive, splendidly, ensuring that any remnants of the conquered are rapidly starved of earth and light, disappearing forever. The force is evident in every square foot of earth left unmowed and among the surviving apple trees, where a dense monoculture of goldenrod has taken up residence. (Who says natives cannot also be invasive?) At the same time, fungi and bacteria are busily breaking down the old apple trees, making room for whatever has already subjugated the ground below them. As the trees die, stands of young poplars grow in straight ranks. Blueberries, low-bush, appeared one year on the rocky east slope. With their white-cupped flowers and promise of intense tiny fruit, a miracle! But within two summers the blackberries spread over them, expanding from delicate sprouts to insurmountable mats, demanding the elimination of the delicate competition. It was clear that the native blueberries, meekly hugging the boulders, will be vanquished by the viciously thorned, non-native blackberries. But one day, the blackberries themselves will be overcome by the shade of the encroaching forest. Native or not, invasive or not, every species will eventually be replaced by another, just as land left alone reverts to forest. I was dumbfounded to learn only recently that the most heavily forested region in the United States is not the Rockies, as I always assumed, but the Northeast, a huge swath of land stretching through the Catskills, Taconics, and Adirondacks to the White Mountains and the mountains of Maine, all the way to the Atlantic. This region, some of it heavily populated, remains more than 80 percent forested.

In the Northeast, the force is with the forest.

We are not ready to give in to natural succession. On this tiny spot of earth, we are determined to disrupt it, at least for now. The meadow will reign. Not just for our pleasure either; this meadow is a diversity hotspot, a home to countless pollinators and ground-nesting birds in desperate need of homes.

The more I learn, though, the more I realize that all our learning and backbreaking work are strictly a finger in the dike. Because in addition to natural succession, we are dealing with climate change. And climate change is a boon to invasive species, especially in the Northeast. Southern states host more invasive species than northern areas, but over the next few decades, many of them will move north, toward us, as our climate becomes more hospitable. Vermont is projected to get seventy-five to one hundred new invasive plants by 2050. Kudzu has already made its appearance in Connecticut and Massachusetts. Our cold winters have kept kudzu from moving this far north, but not for long. I keep hearing from old-timers about thirty-below temperatures for weeks and deep snow on the ground from October to April. Our winters now are considerably milder.

"Climate change can favor nonnative invading species over native ones. Extreme weather events aid species invasions by decreasing native communities' resistance to their establishment and by occasionally putting native species at a competitive disadvantage. . . . Climate change can also facilitate species invasions through physiological impacts, such as by increasing reproduction and growth rates," states a report from the 2017 Northeast Climate Impacts Assessment.

And there's more. The non-native flowers adjusted their flowering time depending on the temperature; in warmer years they flowered earlier, while in cooler years they flowered later. Native species tended to flower at the same time every year, regardless of the rising temperatures. How can we blame the newcomers for being better competitors?

Another group of researchers from Harvard University confirmed what the first group found in Thoreau's woods. Invasive non-native species flowered eleven days earlier than native species, and nine days earlier than non-native species that weren't classified as invasive.

It's not only earlier spring that gives invasive non-natives an advantage; longer autumns also benefit them. They evolve rapidly to respond to warmer temperatures and later freezing events by dropping their leaves later, in effect having a longer growing season than the natives that are not evolving as rapidly. Furthermore, insect pests are also able to take advantage of warmer autumns by speeding development and delaying diapause, in effect producing more generations and more insects to attack our native plants.

Finally, as $CO_2$ in the atmosphere continues to increase as a byproduct of burning fossil fuels, tests show that weeds respond more positively (read: grow bigger and faster, and spread more) to increases in carbon dioxide than native species and agricultural crops.

All this strikes fear and loathing in my heart, especially this throwaway line in the same report: "Rising $CO_2$ spurs root growth in Canada thistle"! The rate of change is not mentioned, but I also learn that dandelions evolve in a single season to take advantage of the $CO_2$-enhanced atmosphere. I can live with improved dandelions, but speeded-up root growth in thistle is thistle on testosterone, unnatural, a vegetable terror.

It's true though. Weeds are simply better equipped to cope with *and* to take advantage of environmental change.

"When you change a resource in the environment you are going to, in effect, favor the weed over the crop," explains Lewis Ziska, a plant physiologist. It better be a very steep and rapid learning curve for natives, or else!

And just when I thought I knew all I needed to about weeds' outrageous adaptability, I found this: "Several studies suggest that the ongoing rise in the air's $CO_2$ content likely will *not* favor the growth of weedy species over that of crops and native plants. In fact, it may well provide non-weeds greater protection against weed-induced decreases in their productivity and growth. Thus, future increases in the air's $CO_2$ content may actually increase the competitiveness of non-weeds over weeds."

Poring over this conflicting information, I realize that it doesn't matter all that much whether weeds benefit from increased $CO_2$ or not. Ten thousand years of coexistence with us has created superplants that will flourish no matter what we do to them. We can hoe, pull, burn, spray, curse, and chop. Weeds have adapted to every means we use to exterminate them. Some even turn our extermination attempts to their own advantage. Destroying thistle aboveground only encourages its underground system—now enhanced with bits of severed root—to sprout bigger, wider, more powerfully. The industrial chemicals that work best in agricultural settings, where they are sprayed over large areas, have serious downsides, killing not just their target but the birds and insects that feed on the plants, contaminating nearby water and poisoning the soil. And they even these lose their effectiveness over time, as the plants—over five hundred weeds at present—realize they must do something to survive, and develop resistance to the chemicals. In fact, preliminary studies show that the effectiveness of herbicides drops in direct proportion to the increase in temperature and $CO_2$. And plants can develop cross-resistance—a reaction in which exposure to one herbicide produces resistance to other, completely different chemicals.

Cities, states, whole countries are busily involved in eradication efforts, but even such huge, concerted movement is mostly doomed to failure.

The New York City Department of Parks and Recreation has spent almost a million dollars treating just thirty acres of knotweed since 2010. The plant got its start in New York City around the turn of the twentieth century, when it was tried out in the New York Botanical Garden. And unlike kudzu and pigweed, which have already invaded most of the territory they will take over, knotweed is still in the early stages of invasion. Apparently, it has much more territory to conquer.

The Bureau of Land Management manages 245 million acres of public lands, primarily in the western United States and Alaska. Of these, seventy-nine million are "infested" with invasive weeds. America's private ranchers spend five billion per year to try to control weeds, according to the Bureau of Land Management website. The United States spends $137 billion annually to combat weeds; worldwide, that number adds up to an astounding $1.4 trillion. That's 5 percent of the global economy!

These numbers don't include the cost involved in combating invasive animals on land, sea and lakes, where there are actually some impressive success stories. But the victories have pretty much been limited to large mammals such as pigs and goats in the Galapagos, and rodents, goats, and feral cats on other islands. These efforts involved enormous financial expenditures, took many years, and were fought in the contained space of islands. These successes don't readily translate to plants on continents.

In *Beyond the War on Invasive Species*, Tao Orion describes the first attempts to restore a wetland in Oregon's Willamette Valley:

> *The plan . . . called for the removal of 30,000 dump truck loads of soil—enough to fill a football stadium 330 feet deep—in order to reach the water table and create year-round standing water. Bulldozers, scrapers, excavators, and dump trucks rolled over the site day after day, for months on end, digging, shaping, compacting the soil. The site was sprayed and sprayed again. Thousands of pounds of native seeds were broadcast . . . and yet invasive species still thrived while little of the native seeds germinated. It turns out they were not well adapted to grow in bulldozer tracks and clay subsoil, while the invasive plants thrived in this difficult environment.*

Controlling invasives in public areas presents different problems. Giant machinery or people decked out with big biohazard suits spraying plants in public parks makes for a bad image. So some dozen cities have turned to goats to control invasive woody plants in public parks. In Pittsburgh the animals eat porcelain berry vines. In Minneapolis they chew down buckthorn. In New York City they nibble on English ivy, and in Southern California they clear brush. Surely as close to a natural control as one can get.

But natural controls have been known to backfire.

In *Where Do Camels Belong?* Ken Thompson writes about an attempt to control knapweed with two European flies that lay their eggs in the flower heads, reducing its seed production and thereby slashing the number of future plants. But very soon the fly larvae became a favorite food of deer mice, which along with the larvae also consumed the seeds, which they then deposited widely (read: planted) with their dung. And then the great horned owls, which ate the mice, which contained the seeds, dispersed the seed ever farther. This story is like a cumulative song, popular in many cultures, in which each verse repeats the previous verse and adds a new element, so that the verses become progressively longer as the mayhem grows. It turns out that only one in three species introduced as biological controls gets established in its new environment, and only half of those control the intended enemy.

But some biological controls are spectacularly successful, like the one that is laying purple loosestrife low, the very plant described as "invader, pest, menace, plague, killer, scourge, monster, public enemy number one, enemy of wildlife, time bomb, disaster, nightmare, rogue, strangler, barbarian and the Freddy Krueger of plants." Various beetles are now munching away at the plant's stems, leaves, and roots, reducing its population to manageable levels. Experiments are underway with a root-crown mining weevil that may destroy garlic mustard, and with a gall-forming weevil to control yellow toadflax. Until recently, I thought toadflax was a pretty wildflower in our meadow. Which just goes to show how easily the division between weeds and wildflowers can be upended.

Seeds of invasive weeds survive in the soil for decades. (Some seeds can live for hundreds, thousands of years. Seven date palm trees have been grown from two-thousand-year-old seeds that were found in the Judean desert near Jerusalem.) What this means is that there are many more mysterious and unwanted plants waiting to sprout and be noticed over the years we'll be living on this hill. The seeds of the weeds I am waging war on today may have been sleeping in the earth long before we moved here. They are an ancestral presence, immortal. I didn't know any of this. It took years to educate my eyes, to make them see the vortex of old and new life under the stillness of the earth's surface.

Optimists believe eradication is possible, but by now there are not many optimists left. Realists know eradication is "more like a down payment with further installments that continue indefinitely."

So what have I been doing, moving up and down the hill in overlapping lines for the past four hours, sweaty in long sleeves and long socks, the sprayer heavy on my back, hurting my shoulders, my cramped fingers wrapped around the nozzle and my heart spraying vengeance?

Is it hopeless then? Will it be "nature" or weeds? Weeds or us? Weeds and nature and us?

By this point in my weed odyssey, I have reached a new plateau of grudging acceptance defined by a firm red line. I am ready to entertain multiple visions of how the future might unfold.

First, I realize, it makes no sense for any organism to multiply ad infinitum. Any animal (except humans) or plant that did that would ensure its own demise. Animals, including our squirrels here, have mast years when food is plentiful and as a result their population grows. But the following year is usually one of want, when the trees produce less seeds and nuts, and the squirrel population is brought back to a manageable level. A plant or animal that kept expanding exponentially would soon use up all available resources, whether it needs acorns, water, or soil to survive.

But no plant would be allowed to even try to endlessly propagate, at least not in the long term. Because plants have not populated the earth, outnumbering all other life, and survived for millions of years without developing coping mechanisms for just such a scenario. And this talent continues to be deployed against threatening plants. In the short term, it may appear to us that the natives are or will be shortly vanquished, but over time the natives and non-natives will reach an equilibrium. As was shown in the regenerating forests of Puerto Rico, where new forests have risen from the wreckage, and in Ohio, where the invasive weeds simply vanished over time.

A University of Georgia study shows how this scenario can unfold. Garlic mustard—the forest equivalent of our charlock—

wages chemical warfare with a compound known as sinigrin. Sinigrin kills the fungi that help native plants extract nutrients from the soil. Furthermore, garlic mustard increases its sinigrin output where more local plants are present. Meanwhile, the local plants, specifically the clearweed that was chosen for this study, show higher levels of resistance to sinigrin in areas where the two species have a longer history of growing together. In other words, the local clearweed is evolving in response to the invader, the study's author notes.

Another plant, called fritillaria, a pretty wildflower that grows from a bulb among the jumbled scree in the Himalayas, has been popular in Chinese medicine for thousands of years. But as demand increases, the plant becomes increasingly harder to spot. It has turned its leaves from bright green into a dull brown, in effect adapting camouflage.

Invasive plants are rarely threatened by the insects or diseases that attack native plants. But over time, less picky insects may develop a taste for the invasives. And while the natives have had eons to develop defenses against the same attackers, the newly arrived will find themselves defenseless.

Animals have also been found to undergo rapid evolution. As snow cover declines, tawny owls in Finland are turning darker. Atlantic killifish in New Jersey's Newark Bay, infamous for its toxic waters, have returned despite their sensitivity to the dioxin and PCBs that pollute the water. It seems the fish have evolved adaptations that make them up to eight thousand times more resistant to the pollutants. These kinds of changes are happening at an astoundingly rapid pace. While cheatgrass and fritillaria's changes are less dramatic, they are indicative of plants' equally astounding ability to adapt.

All of this is logical. From an evolutionary perspective, it simply makes sense for species to live in equilibrium and fit into their environment. Once again, the glaring exception is us humans. We continue to overrun the earth, making us *the* most invasive species on the planet.

In some cases, we can help reach the desired equilibrium without outright war. One sure way to decimate the plants we don't want is to use them for our own needs. Has anyone considered turning kudzu—"the plant that ate the South"—into fuel? Why grow corn with great expenditures of labor, machinery, and petroleum-based fertilizers to produce ethanol? Why not turn to kudzu? Its roots are as much as 50 percent starch by weight, its vines can grow a foot a day, and both are there for the taking. There are likely other invasive candidates also just waiting for discovery of their potential.

With climate change and the uncertain future that entails, weeds may become the answer to feeding ourselves. Wild relatives of our cultivated crops possess diverse genomes that often provide the needed resistance. After a million people died of starvation, the Irish potato blight was solved by finding a wild (weedy) relative that was resistant to the blight.

If all else fails—and even if it doesn't—we could just eat our invasives! This is hardly a revolutionary idea. Dandelion greens are sold in ordinary food markets in my small Vermont city, and our backyards are loaded with invasive edibles, from wild onions and cress to burdock root and garlic mustard. Young knotweed and pokeweed shoots are starting to appear in sophisticated food markets, as are lavish cookbooks on cooking wild. And why not? Eating invasive weeds, like turning them into fuel to power our vehicles, is a win-win—for humans at least.

Sometimes I view the meadow as I once viewed my unruly hair.

I came of age in the era when long, straight, preferably blond hair, parted in the middle, was de rigueur for any white girl under thirty. Mine was neither straight nor blond, nor would it even take a proper part, in the middle or anywhere else. Years spent trying to tame it into some simulation of what was acceptable proved futile. At some point, I started bargaining with the hair gods. I was willing to settle for a part with straight hair on top. Or even just straight bangs that would fly around in breezes and settle back attractively into their former position. It didn't work, and in time, my hair and I reached a sort of conciliation interspersed with regular flare-ups.

In a similar process, I have come to accept that the meadow will never live up to the perfection I imagined. Living on this harsh hill by ourselves, we have watched hurricane-size clouds rush up from the valley, seen blizzards bury trees up to their lowest branches, and heard windstorms tear tiles off the roof. All this, while we stood around helplessly, wondering where we would take cover if needed in a glass house with no basement. This hill has proved what we are told but rarely experience: that nature is all-powerful and I am inconsequential. That the power of the meadow is in its self-willed nature and its ability to regenerate at will. And that to survive, I, too, must be "adaptable to change," in Darwin's words.

In adapting, I try to be both tenacious and flexible. All weeds, including non-native invasive weeds, are not created equal. Nor are they just lovely plants growing in the wrong place. There are those that can be allowed to continue to live out their lives peacefully in the meadow. I will not try to eradicate the wild madder or the bindweed because they are not bent on conquering all. I will let the poplars and boxelders live and grow because they stay in their designated locations, where we encourage nature to take its course. And I have reached a rapprochement with all the other uninvited but acceptable guests who are rapidly becoming permanent residents, on their way to full citizenship.

But I cannot accept looking out at a field of rampaging thistles and poisonous parsnips. We will eradicate them from the parts of the meadow that are visible from where we watch the sun rise and set, where we walk to the mailbox, or sit in the

Adirondack chairs to read or to dream. Here we will continue to yank, dig, pull, spray, and cut for as long as it takes.

The rest of the meadow will get my attention but not my obsession. We will try out various methods for as long as strength and pocketbook allow. Humbled, I am ready to accept far less than total victory. A cold peace, a workable accommodation will suffice. Let the invasives live as long as they let the meadow live. My will is not the only one that matters here; everything that grows here also has a will and a way.

"Tell me the landscape in which you live and I will tell you who you are," the philosopher José Ortega y Gasset is known to have said. I don't know the context, but I interpret it to mean that character is formed, at least in part, by the physical landscape in which one lives life. This is underscored by the fact that at one time people and places were synonymous: Sappho of Lesbos, for example. Or Saint Francis of Assisi. Jesus of Nazareth.

Research suggests that mountainous landscapes may promote openness to new experiences among the people who live in them. The study authors also reported that these same people scored lower for traits such as agreeableness and extroversion, in keeping with the stereotype of the laconic individualist that has often been portrayed in Westerns. The spirit of adventure seems to come with an embrace of solitude and isolation, all traits that may help adaptation to these harsh environments. These findings were confirmed by researchers at the University of Virginia, whose work showed that introverts did indeed prefer mountains and were happier in wooded rather than in open areas. Extroverts gravitated to beaches with open views and opportunities to see people.

People with personality traits that include agreeableness and conscientiousness are drawn to landscapes featuring vast expanses and views, and less so to landscapes characterized by enclosed, protected spaces.

It appears then that Ortega y Gasset's pronouncement is being confirmed by research many decades later. Personality traits determine which landscapes we are attracted to. What I wonder about is how the landscape in which we find ourselves—by choice or happenstance—changes us.

Our huge sky, open land, and distant views met my fantasies of the perfect landscape. I may even fit the personality traits described. Inhabiting this world has allowed the sky, the moonrise, the scouring winds, and the meadow and all its denizens to inhabit and change me. Physical labor coupled with miles of walking up and down the hill has resulted in fitness. The meadow's many mysteries have driven me to learn to read the land until I am slowly becoming a budding botanist. The shifting skyscape has opened new interests in worlds beyond our earth. Growing food has provided more than sun-warmed tomatoes and redolent herbs; there is the daily gratitude I try to remember to offer to the earth, the sun, the rain. Being present every day is a privilege that allows me to observe the smallest incremental changes. To be astonished over and over. At the magical promise of a tiny seed that has the self-knowledge to become leaf, stem, flower, fruit. At the power of the whole meadow to rise from death to pulsating life every spring. At the forests that each spring turn from dead gray to red and then burst into fifty shades of green, so many more greens than the English language has words to describe. Watching a storm pass from horizon to horizon is soul expanding. The slaps of icy or hot winds are cleansing. Solitude and silence are braided into my days.

Occasionally, feeling reverent, I reach a state of awe for the green flame of this world, and then, for a moment, I am timeless and mindless, yet fully present and connected to all the life under me, around me, above me, and I feel humbled, aware of my human limitations. But as I grow smaller in the immensity of the world, there is a kind of glory in just being in it. This spot in the world has entered my soul and shifted the arc of my life.

But day to day, the meadow and I remain locked in an uncomfortable embrace. Every day I wrestle with it. On some days, I wrestle meaning from it that shapes my understanding of life—mine and the meadow's—as a process of continual change.

What we are seeing as we walk the paths in the meadow is merely a snapshot in time, capturing an immeasurably brief moment. The seeds of the grasses and asters were here well before we came to see the dying orchard. They were here before the orchard, when this hilltop was a field where cows grazed, and before that when white sheep dotted the grass. And back when this was a forest of pines and maples hundreds of feet high. The pines and maples were then the newcomers, the ones that replaced the earlier grasses and mosses growing on what had not long before been ice-scoured new earth left by retreating glaciers. The glaciers themselves were the result of only the latest major climate shift. Before the series of glaciers that erased life in the Northern Hemisphere, there were palm trees in Alaska, crocodiles in the Arctic, and Lake Champlain was a tropical sea.

With each ice age, plants moved great distances because they had to and because it's easier and faster to migrate than to evolve. Wherever plants moved, they created "nature." Everything alive here today is here because plants grew and made seeds that grew into new plants, which grew and sometimes evolved into something new and wonderful or something destructive but possibly necessary and certainly "natural." Even today, when our human footprint is enormous, nature not only survives but remains beautiful, complex, vital. I have neither the ability nor the right to interfere in this process—except in a few select cases and for only so long.

We don't know what miracles lurk in the genes of what lives today, nor how these miracles will create another kind of nature, because change is in the genes of everything that lives. This meadow will soon become something else. Time will erase all trace of us and our work, without ill will or intent. The land will become what it was meant to be. We won't live to see this because our human time on this tiny spot of earth is immeasurably short; we will be gone in less than a blink of geologic time. But evolution will march on. Nature will evolve into a different nature. Humans will be supplanted by . . . what? I would place my bet on crows. Having spent many hours watching them, I am convinced their intelligence is not far behind ours. Our demise would give them the chance to evolve into *Corvus sapiens.*

For now, I try to look around instead of ahead. We are creating beauty for us and abundance for all that lives in this meadow. That is a positive act, an act of defiance in the face of all that is wrong with the world. It's as good a way to spend our days as any. I continue to play god in the meadow, but I will try to be a more modest, more respectful, accepting, and more forgiving god, one with a longer perspective.

# ACKNOWLEDGMENTS

I am grateful to my family and friends for their support and encouragement. I am especially thankful to my husband, Ted, for his partnership in the labor of (mostly) love in the meadow and his tolerance for my endless hours of reading and writing; to the six special women in my writing group who offered many intelligent ideas, as well as to Elaine Auerbach, author and friend, whose close reading was especially helpful; to my children, who despite very busy lives take great interest and pride in their mother's work; to my editor Brian Halley and his faith in the project; to the many experts I spoke with who willingly gave of their time and knowledge, and the many experts I never spoke with but who shared their vast learning on paper and on the Internet. And finally, to the meadow and its myriad plant and animal denizens, each and every one a marvel that never fails to arouse curiosity and admiration.

# NOTES

PG# 1: FROM ORCHARD TO MEADOW

3 ***wiping out thousands of trees:*** Jim Robbins, "Fire Blight Spreads Northward, Threatening Apple Orchards," *New York Times*, December 2, 2019.

8 ***a massive decline:*** American Birding Association, https://www.aba.org/bobolink-conservation/.

11 ***the bobolinks' shrinking numbers:*** "Red-Winged Blackbird," American Bird Conservancy, accessed November 15, 2021, https://abcbirds.org/bird/red-winged-blackbird.

2: BUGS

15 ***higher than becoming unemployed or getting mugged:*** "American's Top Fears 2016: Chapman University Survey of American Fears," Voice of Wilkinson, Chapman University, October 11, 2016, https://blogs.chapman.edu/wilkinson/2016/10/11/americas-top-fears-2016/.

***a service worth as much as $577 billion every year:*** "The Value of Pollinators to the Ecosystem and Our Economy," *Forbes*, October 14, 2019, https://www.forbes.com/sites/bayer/2019/10/14/the-value-of-pollinators-to-the-ecosystem-and-our-economy/?sh=29487327a1d6.

***insects populations are in free fall:*** Brooke Jarvis, "The Insect Apocalypse Is Here," *New York Times*, November 27, 2018.

4: WISDOM

29 ***Plants dominate every terrestrial environment:*** Brian Resnick and Javier Zarracina, "All Line in Earth in One Staggering Chart," *Vox*, August 15, 2018, https://www.vox.com/science-and-health/2018/5/29/17386112/all-life-on-earth-chart-weight-plants-animals-pnas.

30 ***"a set of relationships, not individuals":*** David George Haskell, *The Songs of Trees: Stories from Nature's Great Connectors* (New York: Viking, 2017), 38–39.

5: THE ADVANCE GUARD

42 ***sixteen million Genghis Khan descendants living today:*** David Hilary Mayell, "Genghis Khan a Prolific Lover, DNA Data Implies," *National Geographic*, February 14, 2003.

8: WISDOM II

62 ***to create more life out of death:*** David R. Montgomery and Anne Biklé, *The Hidden Half of Nature: The Microbial Roots of Life and Health* (New York: W. W. Norton, 2016), 93.

***they would stretch one hundred million light-years:*** Montgomery and Biklé, *Hidden Half of Nature*, 24.

63 ***Even rock can serve as food to these ancient life forms:*** Jules Bernstein, "Let Them Eat Rocks," *UC California Riverside News*, September 23, 2020.

9: SPEAKING OF IMMORTALITY

71 ***the hogweed population is expanding by 10 percent a year:*** Maria Antonova, "A Toxic Alien Is Taking Over Russia," *New York Times*, October 3, 2020.

***"salutary scourges of human arrogance":*** Richard Mabey, *Weeds: In Defense of Nature's Most Unloved Plants* (New York: Harper Collins, 2010), 155.

72 ***"sprouting wherever they went":*** Michael Pollan, "Weeds Are Us," *New York Times*, November 5, 1989.

***non-native grasses:*** Pollan, "Weeds Are Us."

11: TOXIC ALIENS TAKING OVER!

78 ***"has led to my growing madness":*** Henry Grabar, "Oh No, Not Knoweed!" Slate.com, May 8, 2019, https://slate.com/technology/2019/05/japanese-knotweed-invasive-plants.html.

80 ***"what forms of life shall be preserved":*** Jedediah Purdy, "Environmentalism's Racist History," *New Yorker*, August 13, 2015.

82 ***The quotas remained in place until the late 1950s:*** Colin Woodward, *American Nations: A History of the Eleven Rival Regional Cultures of North America* (New York: Penguin Books, 2012), 255.

***"the beauty of our home forest, is at stake":*** Stephen Jay Gould, "An Evolutionary Perspective on Strengths, Fallacies and Confusions in the Concept of Native Plants," *Arnoldia* 58, no. 1 (February 15, 1998): 3–10.

85 ***a particular "fitness":*** Anjali Vaidya, "Native or Invasive?," *Orion*, March/April 2017.

***Alien species are alien in name only:*** Alan Burdick, "The Truth about Invasive Species," *Discover*, January 19, 2005.

86 ***the common description of thistle:*** "Field Guide for Managing Thistle in the Southwest," USDA, September 2014, https://www.fs.usda.gov/Internet/FSE_DOCUMENTS/stelprdb5410109.pdf.

13: WHO WILL LIVE AND WHO WILL DIE?

95 ***at the root of racism even today:*** "Linneause and Race," Linnaean Society of London, accessed November 15, 2021, https://www.linnean.org/learning/who-was-linnaeus/linnaeus-and-race.

***a definition we still use today:*** Ken Thompson, *Where Do Camels Belong? The Story and Science of Invasive Species* (London: Profile Books, 2014), 32.

***Watson didn't attach any value judgment:*** Thompson, *Where Do Camels Belong?*, 32.

101 ***"indigenous populations in the past were more numerous":*** Ben Panko, "The Supposedly Pristine, Untouched Amazon Rainforest Was Actually Shaped by Humans," *Smithsonian Magazine*, March 3, 2017.

102 ***human impact on places considered untouched:*** Fred Pearce, *The New Wild: Why Invasive Species Will Be Nature's Salvation* (Boston: Beacon Press, 2015), 122.

***the landscape was "unkempt":*** Larry Weaner, New Directions in the American Landscape webinar, June 3, 2020.

104 ***a very efficient carbon sink:*** Elizabeth A. Kellogg, "C4 Photosynthesis," *Current Biology* 23, no. 14 (July 2013): R594–R599.

105 ***over the course of earth's history:*** Anjali Vaidya, "Native or Invasive?," *Orion*, March/April 2017.

15: STALKING THE EXPERTS

109 ***the guru of meadows:*** Larry Weaner, "Native Meadows: Let's Get Real!" New Directions in American Landscape webinar, March 19, 2021 (recording no longer available).

112 ***increase their resistance to herbicides:*** Maor Matrzafi of Newe Ya'ar Research Center, Israel, at Northeast RISCC, "Management: Invasive Species & Climate Change Symposium," January 21, 2021.

113–114 ***Mason bees . . . are extraordinary pollinators:*** Judy Beaudette, "Attract Mason Bees—No Protective Gear Needed," *Ecological Landscaping*, March 15, 2013.

16: THE SHAKESPEARE GARDEN

122 ***over two hundred species of birds:*** "In Conversation with Ornithologist and Author Scott Weidensaul on Bird Migration," April 22, 2021, accessed November 20, 2021, https://www.centralparknyc.org/articles/in-conversation-with-scott-weidensaul.

17: IN WHICH WE REACH AN IMPASSE

128 ***"Death by a Thousand Cuts":*** David L. Wagner, Eliza M. Grames, Mathew L. Forister, May R. Berenbaum, and David Stopak, "Insect Decline in the Anthropocene: Death by a Thousand Cuts," Proceedings of the National Academies of Science (PNAS), January 12, 2020.

129 ***a precious asset:*** Angela Laws, "Mitigating the Effects of Climate Change on Grassland Butterflies," *Wings: The Magazine of Xerces Society*, September 3, 2020.

130 ***bouquets of non-native invasive weeds:*** Rebecca A. Fletcher, Rachel K. Brooks, Vasiliy T. Lakoba, Gourav Sharma, Ariel R. Heminger, Christopher C. Dickinson, and Jacob N. Barney, "Invasive Plants Negatively Impact Native, But Not Exotic, Animals," *Global Change Biology*, August 7, 2019, photo on WVTF Radio webpage, September 27, 2019, accessed November 20, 2021, https://www.wvtf.org/news/2019-09-27/pretty-poison-vt-study-first-to-confirm-invasive-plants-threaten-native-wildlife#stream/0.

19: HOW TO BECOME NATIVE

135 ***They had become American:*** Colin Woodard, *American Nations: A History of the Eleven Rival Regional Cultures of North America* (London: Penguin, 2011), 259.

136 ***A third of residential water use:*** EPA estimate of water use, accessed November 20, 2021, https://19january2017snapshot.epa.gov/www3/watersense/pubs/outdoor.html.

***"lawns are a useless vestige of a bygone era":*** Joe Queenan, "Let's Get Rid of All the Lawns," *Wall Street Journal*, April 24, 2015.

138 ***Eventually, though, they die:*** Ken Thompson, *Where Do Camels Belong? The Story and Science of Invasive Species* (London: Profile Books, 2014), 9–10.

20: REALLY?

140 ***How could it look anything but magnificent:*** Emma Marris, "Urban Wilderness and the High Line Problem," *Urban Landscaping*, October 5, 2020.

141 ***"Designed meadows have been available for years":*** Larry Weaner, "Native Meadows: Let's Get Real!" New Directions in American Landscape webinar, March 19, 2021 (recording no longer available).

## 21: THE FIRST AND PRESENT BEAUTY

146 ***"invasive species may be creating a new one":*** Garry Hamilton, *Super Species: The Species That Will Dominate the Planet* (Boston: Firefly Books, 2010), 181.

147 ***functioning biodiverse natural ecosystems:*** Hamilton, *Super Species*, 181.

***have finally caught up with them as well:*** Ken Thompson, *Where Do Camels Belong? The Story and Science of Invasive Species* (London: Profile Books, 2014), 157.

148 ***wild animals rarely die of old age anyway:*** Fred Pearce, *The New Wild: Why Invasive Species Will Be Nature's Salvation* (Boston: Beacon Press, 2015), 175.

***two thousand non-native plants:*** Pearce, *New Wild*, 112–13.

***established ecosystems . . . are able to absorb non-natives:*** James H. Brown and Dov F. Sax, "Aliens among Us," *Conservation* 8, no. 2 (July 29, 2008): https://www.conservationmagazine.org/2008/07/aliens-among-us/.

***"They have no preordained template. No guest list":*** Pearce, *New Wild*, 159.

149 ***making it possible for the native flowers, grasses, and wildlife to survive:*** Tom Christopher, "Can Weeds Help Solve the Climate Crisis?," *New York Times*, June 30, 2008.

150 ***increasing poverty at one end and affluence on the other:*** Nicola Seitz, Dennis vanEngelsdorp, and Sara D. Leonhardt, "Are Native and Non-Native Pollinator Friendly Plants Equally Valuable for Native Wild Bee Communities?," *Ecology and Evolution* 10, no. 23 (December 2020): 12838–50.

***this is an extremely valuable service:*** Christopher, "Can Weeds Help?"

***scientists created a more robust, disease-resistant domesticated oat:*** Maor Matzrafi, "Climate Change Exacerbates the Damage of Invasive Weed Species through Reduced Herbicide Efficacy," Northeast RISCC, "Management: Invasive Species & Climate Change Symposium," January 21, 2021, https://www.risccnetwork.org/symposia-2021-presentations.

151 ***boosting harvests to feed a growing population:*** Fourth National Climate Assessment, 2017, accessed November 20, 2021, https://nca2018.globalchange.gov/chapter/7/.

***That much carbon removed from the atmosphere could . . . save the world:*** Audrey Clark, "Invasive Plants on the Rise in Vermont," *Vermont Digger*, September 2, 2013.

152 ***"The human soul is hungry for beauty":*** John O'Donohue, *Beauty: The Invisible Embrace* (New York: Harper, 2005).

## 23: THE SWEET SPOT

157 ***Vermont is projected to get seventy-five to one hundred new invasive plants by 2050:*** Peter C. Frumhoff et al., "Confronting Climate Change in the U.S. Northeast," Union of Concerned Scientists, July 2007.

158 ***"increasing reproduction and growth rates":*** Frumhoff et al., "Confronting Climate Change."

***flower at the same time every year:*** Tom Christopher, "Can Weeds Help Solve the Climate Crisis?," *New York Times*, June 30, 2008.

***Invasive non-native species flowered eleven days earlier:*** Holly Metter, "Records Dating Back to Thoreau Show Some Sharp Shifts in Plant Flowering near Walden Pond: Effects of Climate Change Vary Greatly across Plant Families," *Harvard Gazette*, October 28, 2008.

***more insects to attack our native plants:*** Amanda S. Gallinat, Richard B. Primack, and David L. Wagner, "Autumn, the Neglected Season in Climate Change Research," *Cell Press*, February 3, 2015, https://concordmuseum.org/wp-content/uploads/2018/03/Autumn-the-neglected-season-in-climate-change-research.pdf.

159 ***"Rising CO2 spurs root growth in Canada thistle":*** Chris Bright, *Life Out of Bounds: Bioinvasion in a Borderless World* (New York: W. W. Norton, 1998), 53.

***dandelions . . . take advantage of the CO2-enhanced atmosphere:*** "Morning Edition," National Public Radio, July 12, 2007, accessed November 21, 2021, https://www.npr.org/templates/story/story.php?storyId=11903786.

***"favor the weed over the crop":*** Lewis Ziska, cited in Christopher, "Can Weeds Help?"

***"increase the competitiveness of non-weeds over weeds":*** Maor Mitzrahi et al., "Increased Temperatures and Elevated CO2 Levels Reduce the Sensitivity of *Conyza Canadensis* and *Chenopodium Abum* to Glyphosate," *Nature*, February 18, 2019.

160 ***develop resistance to the chemicals:*** International Herbicide-Resistant Weed Database, *Weed Science*, February 2, 2021, https://www.weedscience.org/Home.aspx.

***in direct proportion to the increase in temperature and CO2:*** Robert Naczi, a curator of North American botany at the New York Botanical Garden, quoted in *Slate*, May 8, 2020.

***other, completely different chemicals:*** "Multiple Herbicide-Resistant Weeds and Challenges Ahead," *Cropwatch*, November 19, 2021, Institute of Agriculture and Natural Resources, University of Nebraska–Lincoln, accessed December 6, 2021, https://cropwatch.unl.edu/multiple-herbicide-resistant-weeds-and-challenges-ahead.

***it has much more territory to conquer:*** Tao Orion, *Beyond the War on Invasive Species: A Permaculture Approach to Ecosystem Restoration* (White River Junction, VT: Chelsea Green Publishing, 2015), 6–7.

***That's 5 percent of the global economy:*** Ken Thompson, *Where Do Camels Belong? The Story and Science of Invasive Species* (London: Profile Books, 2014), 46.

161 ***fought in the contained space of islands:*** Thompson, *Where Do Camels Belong?*, 130–35.

***"The plan . . . called for the removal of 30,000":*** Orion, *Beyond the War on Invasive Species*, 6–7.

162 ***dispersed the seed ever farther:*** Thompson, *Where Do Camels Belong?*, 146–47.

***only half of those control the intended enemy:*** Thompson, *Where Do Camels Belong?*, 151.

***"the Freddy Krueger of plants":*** Courtney L. J. Rowe and Elizabeth A. Leger, "Competitive Seedlings and Inherited Traits: A Test of Rapid Evolution of *Elymus multisetus* (Big Squirreltail)," *Evolutionary Applications*, October 29, 2010.

***"more like a down payment with further installments that continue indefinitely":*** Thompson, *Where Do Camels Belong?*, 135.

164 ***the local clearweed is evolving in response to the invader:*** "Native Species Fight Back: First Evidence of Coevolution between Invasive, Native Species," *Science Daily*, June 28, 2012, accessed December 6, 2021, https://www.sciencedaily.com/releases/2012/06/120628174536.htm.

***in effect adapting camouflage:*** Jonathan Lambert, "These Plants Seem Like They're Trying to Hide from People," *Science News*, November 20, 2020, accessed November 21, 2021, https://www.sciencenews.org/article/plant-camouflage-people-china-traditional-medicine-fritillaria.

***the newly arrived will find themselves defenseless:*** Thompson, *Where Do Camels Belong?*, 162.

***tawny owls in Finland are turning darker:*** David Biello, "Climate Change Drives (Micro)Evolution in Finland," *Scientific American*, February 23, 2011.

***happening at an astoundingly rapid pace:*** Joanna Klein, "Rapid Evolution Saved This Fish from Pollution, Study Says," *New York Times*, December 9, 2016.

165 ***lavish cookbooks on cooking wild:*** Marie Viljoen/Saveur, "Ten Weeds You Can Eat," *Popular Science*, April 19, 2020.

167 ***traits that may help adaptation to these harsh environments:*** Emily Willingham, "Mountain Peaks Seem to Shape Personality Traits in the American West," *Scientific American*, September 8, 2020.

***findings were confirmed by researchers at the University of Virginia:*** Shigehiro Oishi, Thomas Talhelm, and Minha Lee, "Personality and Geography: Introverts Prefer Mountains," *Journal of Research in Personality* 58 (October 2015): 55–68.

***landscapes characterized by enclosed, protected spaces:*** John A. Johnson and Lisa A. Feldman, "Evolution of Personality, Mood, and Landscape Preferences," Pennsylvania State University, presented at the Sixth Annual Meeting of the Human Behavior and Evolution Society, Ann Arbor, MI, June 1994.